Fourth Edition

W9-BFT-338

THE BOWLER'S MANUAL

LOU BELLISIMO

JEANINE BENNETT

University of Oregon

PRENTICE-HALL, INC., Englewood Cliffs, New Jersey 07632

Library of Congress Cataloging in Publication Data

Bellisimo, Lou.   (date)
    The bowler's manual.

    1. Bowling.   I. Bennett, Jeanine.   II. Title.
GV903.B4   1982   794.6   81-17834
ISBN   0-13-080507-6   AACR2

Editorial/production supervision by Daniel Mausner
Cover design by Ray Lundgren (Tony Ferrara Studio)
Manufacturing buyer: Harry P. Baisley

Printed in the United States of America

10   9   8   7   6   5   4   3   2   1

ISBN 0-13-080507-6

Prentice-Hall International, Inc., *London*
Prentice-Hall of Australia Pty. Limited, *Sydney*
Prentice-Hall of Canada, Ltd., *Toronto*
Prentice-Hall of India Private Limited, *New Delhi*
Prentice-Hall of Japan, Inc., *Tokyo*
Prentice-Hall of Southeast Asia Pte. Ltd., *Singapore*
Whitehall Books Limited, *Wellington, New Zealand*

CONTENTS

PREFACE   *vii*

I   FUNDAMENTALS FOR THE BEGINNER   1

1. GETTING THE BEGINNER STARTED   *1*

Orientation   *1*
Finding a Ball That Fits   *2*
How to Pick Up a Bowling Ball   *4*
Beginning Techniques for Learning and for Teaching Bowling   *5*
The Stance   *5*
The One-Step Delivery   *10*
The Three-Step Approach Practice Technique   *16*
Instructional Information   *20*

2. THE COMPLETE APPROACH AND DELIVERY   *21*

Changing from the Three-Step to the Four-Step Approach   *21*
Four-Step Approach   *24*
Analysis of the Four-Step Approach   *28*

3.   SPOT, PIN, AND LINE BOWLING   *29*

The Foul Line   *31*
The Ball's Path to the Pins   *31*

4.   PLAYING SPARES   *32*

The Three Basic Spare Angles   *32*

5.   BOWLING ETIQUETTE   *36*

II   THE MECHANICS OF BOWLING   37

6.   TIMING   *37*

Timing in the Approach   *37*
Comparison of Styles   *37*

7.   THREE FUNDAMENTALS FOR DEVELOPING GOOD DELIVERY FORM   *51*

Facing Straight Ahead   *54*
Balance and Leverage   *55*
Straight Pendulum Arm Swing and Follow-Through   *58*
Hand Position   *59*

8.   ANALYSIS OF THE HOOK BALL   *61*

Turn-and-Lift "Cranker"   *66*

9.   PLAYING THE TIGHT LINE   *71*

III   COMMON FAULTS AND HOW TO CORRECT THEM   74

10.   THE THREE INSTRUCTIONAL METHODS   *74*

The Trial Swing   *74*
The Dry Run   *74*
The One-Step Delivery   *75*

11. CORRECTION OF FAULTS: APPROACH   *78*

Approach Timing   *79*
Forcing The Forward Swing   *80*
Ahead of the Ball   *83*
Carrying the Ball   *86*
A Hesitation in the Approach   *88*
A Hop or Rush in the Approach   *89*
Crooked Walk to the Foul Line (Drifting)   *97*

12. CORRECTION OF FAULTS: THE DELIVERY   *98*

Failing to Face Straight Ahead   *98*
Loss of Balance During the Delivery   *103*
Lofting the Ball   *106*
Dropping the Shoulder   *107*
Crooked Pendulum Swing   *108*
Arm Twisting   *100*
The High Backswing   *113*
A Hop in the Delivery   *115*
A Wide Pendulum Swing (Side-Wheeling)   *116*
A Poor Follow-Through   *120*
Ball Speed   *121*
Ball Roll   *121*
Killing the Hook   *123*
Too Much Hook or Curve   *127*
Correcting a Poor Hook   *129*
Correcting the Back-Up   *130*
Over-Turning the Wrist   *131*

IV   TECHNICAL INFORMATION   133

13. TAPS AND SPLITS   *133*

Taps   *133*
Pocket Splits and Deflection   *137*
Other Splits and What to Do About Them   *139*
Which Angle Is Best to Play   *139*

14. DIFFERENT TYPES OF BALL ROLL   *141*

Straight Ball   *141*
Full Roller   *142*
Semi-Roller   *143*
Semi-Spinner   *144*
Full Spinner   *144*
Back-Up and Reverse Hook   *146*
How the Ball Rolls   *147*

15. EQUIPMENT   *147*

16. BALL PITCH   *149*

17. BOWLING LANE SPECIFICATIONS   *151*

18. LANE CONDITIONS   *151*

19. TEACHING SENIOR ADULTS   *152*

20. TEACHING CHILDREN   *154*

21. SCORING THE GAME OF TENPINS   *158*

How to Score a Foul   *160*
Handicaps for Scoring   *160*

22. GLOSSARY FOR BOWLING TERMS AND SLANG   *162*

PREFACE

This book tells you not just how it *should* be done, but how to do it. The basic techniques are explained for the new bowler, and if you are an experienced bowler, you will find many valuable tips about why you may be having trouble and how to make the necessary corrections. The fourth edition of *The Bowler's Manual* pays even more attention to common faults and the three methods bowlers can use to correct them.

None of the pictures—half of them are new to this edition—were posed. They show actual errors and corrections as they occurred.

This manual explains the theory behind each principle, and each section includes tips for self-help in mastering a new idea or in correcting a fault. Individualized instruction is stressed, and each student is encouraged to develop his or her style at an individual pace. Every bowler's style is personal and depends upon many variables, such as general body build, strength, timing, and so on; but each bowler should develop that style within the framework of the proven principles of approach and delivery.

Each page of the first chapter "Fundamentals for the Beginner", has a black dot at the top to identify the section readily.

Our sincere thanks to the many bowlers over the years who have allowed us to analyze their unorthodox styles and habits in order to illustrate points, and to the University of Oregon varsity team members and other students whose invaluable assistance has contributed to the continuing success of this manual. We appreciate the many hours they have spent on this project, both on the lanes and as stagehands helping with equipment.

Special thanks to Jim Hosmer of Eugene, Oregon, for his excellent photography. Acknowledgments and thanks to Jack Anderson, Art Baumohl, Bob Blackley, Robert D. Clark, Jim Ekstrom, A.L. Ellingson, J.J. Kanegae, Tosh Kinjo, Bruce Koppe, and Wayne Wilson.

L.B.
Eugene, Oregon

1

FUNDAMENTALS FOR THE BEGINNER

1. GETTING THE BEGINNER STARTED

Orientation

If you can take three, four, or five steps in a straight line while swinging a bowling ball in an easy pendulum, you can master the game of bowling. To be sure, this is an oversimplification; but the student who time after time can coordinate these two movements—steps and arm swing—has the game eighty percent mastered.

The coordination of these two simple movements is called *timing*. Timing is the simple coordination of the arm swing and the feet. It sounds simple, but it is unquestionably the beginning bowler's largest problem, and on occasion it frustrates even the pros. Good timing allows the bowler to release the ball out beyond the foul line naturally without forcing the swing.

Coordination will be easier for you if you keep in mind at all times to *adjust the steps to fit the swing*, not the swing to fit the steps. Develop a smooth pendulum swing, then fit the necessary number of steps to it.

This first chapter is an orientation lesson that will familiarize you with many aspects of bowling. It presents basic information on selection of the proper ball, mechanics of the approach and delivery, methods of aiming, and other topics that you need to know about before you get started. Scoring the game is explained in chapter 4, which can be read after you have mastered the basics.

A special note to *left-handed bowlers:* By holding up to a mirror the illustrations of right-handed bowlers performing bowling techniques, you can get an image from the perspective that you need in order to bowl left-handed from "your side of the lane."

Finding a Ball That Fits

You do not need to buy special equipment while you are learning to bowl. Bowling establishments furnish bowling balls free and rent shoes at a nominal charge.

Weight. It is important that you select a ball of proper *weight* that fits your hand correctly. Proper selection can make a difference in how well you bowl. Use as heavy a ball as you can comfortably deliver without undue effort or strain. An easy test for proper ball weight is to take a trial swing with the ball. If you can control the ball during the trial swing, you can use it for your regular delivery (the trial swing is a complete practice swing *without* releasing the ball; see figure 7).

Generally, "house" balls are numbered so that their weight can be identified by the number series. For example, balls numbered from 1 to 20 may weigh from 10 to 11 pounds, those numbered from 21 to 30 from 11 to 14 pounds. The American Bowling Congress (A.B.C.) approves weights from 10 to 16 pounds. The Women's International Bowling Congress (W.I.B.C.) allows a maximum of 16 pounds, but specifies no minimum ball weight.

Span. Fully as important as the weight of the ball is the *span*. The span is the distance from the inside edge of the thumb hole to the inside edge of the finger holes. To find a ball with the proper span for you, insert your thumb all the way into the ball. Then stretch your fingers out over the holes. A correct fit must have the center of the second joint one-quarter inch past the inside edge of the finger holes, as illustrated in figure 1.

The holes in the ball should fit snugly enough so that there is no slippage. They should not be so large that your hand or arm must strain in order to maintain

1. The span for the conventional grip

(a) Full fingertip

(b) Semi-fingertip

your grasp of the ball; nor should the holes be so snug that the ball cannot be released.

Grip. The grip in which the fingers are inserted into the ball to the second joint, as described in the section above is called a *conventional grip*. It is the most common and is the only grip recommended for beginners. Balls furnished at bowling establishments will have been drilled for a conventional grip.

You should be aware, however, that there are other types of grips that can be drilled for those who purchase their own equipment. The two most common are the *full fingertip* (figure 2a) and the *semi-fingertip* (figure 2b). These grips are not usually recommended, except for those advanced bowlers who bowl many games each week. The fingers, hand, and arm must be very strong in order to control either of these two grips.

The fingertip and semi-fingertip grips are designed to allow the bowler to apply more hook lift with the fingers at the instant of releasing the ball. As the illustrations show, the span is increased with these grips, which allows the fingers to get a longer and more sustained pull or lift on the finger holes. This, in turn, puts more spin on the ball and consequently more hook. The proper delivery of this type of ball is delicate at best, and the additional hook presents added problems of accuracy. Unfortunately, far too many bowlers, men as well as women, roll the heaviest possible full fingertip. In many cases this cuts down on the amount of control they have of the ball. Because they roll a fingertip does not necessarily mean they have complete control of the ball.

If the ball fits you properly, in a conventional grip, the span for the ring finger will be approximately one-eighth inch longer than the span for the middle finger. Looking at your hand, it appears that the opposite should be true; but by inserting your thumb in the ball, you can see how the ring finger moves farther away from the thumb. Obviously, if a left-hander uses a ball drilled for a right-hander, the span in one of the fingers will be off by about one-quarter inch. The thumb hole should not be too tight, but you should be able to turn the thumb in the thumb hole without much friction. The finger holes should be sufficiently snug to provide a firm grip.

It is impossible for any establishment to stock enough balls to fit everyone. Do the best you can in selecting a house ball, considering weight, span, thumb-hole size, and finger-hole size, in that order. You should purchase your own bowling equipment as soon as possible. You are then sure of proper fit, and the correct equipment will always be available when you want it.

How to Pick Up a Bowling Ball

All bowlers should learn the proper way to pick up a bowling ball. For safety, pick up the ball with both hands on the "side" of the ball, as illustrated in figure 3, to prevent your fingers from getting caught between two bowling balls.

3. Picking up the ball

Beginning Techniques for Learning
and for Teaching Bowling

Bowling is basically a simple game because it consists of two coordinated movements—the swing of the ball and the steps taken in delivering the ball. To be more specific, a bowler develops a smooth, natural arm swing, like the pendulum of a clock, and then adds a certain number of steps to fit this arm swing.

Since bowling first became popular, instructors have labored to find the easiest method to teach these fundamentals to beginners. The several techniques that we have found to be most ideal for developing sound fundamentals, regardless of age or sex of the learner, will be described in the following pages of this section. These are the *trial swing, one-step delivery, dry run, three-step approach,* and finally *four-step approach,* or that number of steps which is most natural to the bowler.

Regardless of the number of steps used later, these techniques, and especially the three-step approach, should be properly practiced until a sound approach, timing, and delivery are mastered. The number of steps used *after* experience is gained should be blended to the natural timing of the full arm swing.

When these practice techniques are understood, most instructors observe that they are a very natural and significant part of the skillful approach and delivery timing. These methods for learning and for teaching encourage a style that includes fundamentals, such as maintaining *balance of the body* and *leverage* as the ball is released, *facing straight ahead,* and developing a *full follow-through.* But perhaps most important, these methods reduce the tendency of many bowlers to force the ball.

Two of the bowlers in figure 4a are left-handed. Since they will step off with the *right* foot, notice they have their weight on the left foot. Both have comfortable positions. The two right-handers likewise have a comfortable stance position. They will be stepping off with the *left* foot, therefore their weight is on the *right* foot.

Since we recommended the three-step approach for beginners, the shorter bowlers will stand approximately 24 inches in front of the 12-foot line of dots. Taller people should stand 12 inches in front.

The Stance

The position in which you hold the ball before the start of the approach to the foul line is called the *stance* or starting position. This stance is also used when you are using the practice techniques that we will be discussing (trial swing, one-step delivery, and so on). For the beginner, we recommend the stance shown in Figure 4. Keep both hands toward the underside of the ball, elbows comfortably close to your sides, and the ball at, or slightly above, waist level. Both feet should be reasonably close together, although the foot supporting the weight of your body may be slightly ahead of the foot that will take the first step in the approach.

4. Starting stance position

Chest-High Stance. When a higher ball position is used in the stance it will generate more momentum during the pendular arm swing. It can, however, interrupt a fluid arm swing (figure 5).

Figure 6 shows a perfectly smooth and easy trial swing from the waist-high stance position.

5. An improperly high stance interrupting a fluid arm swing.

If you are sliding over the foul line while practicing, how far over the line are you sliding? Check the length of your footwork (steps). If it is satisfactory and your timing is good, then move back no more than the distance that you need to correct going over the foul line. If you are finishing your approach short of the foul line (more than 4 to 6 inches), then move closer just the distance that you need to make the correction.

You must also consider your stance position from the left or right side of the approach. It is recommended that the beginning position should be one in which the bowler straddles the board that contains the second spot from the side of the lane bed. For right-handers that is the second dot from the right; generally the fifteen board. For left-handed bowlers it is the second spot from the left. This is the correct position whether you aim directly at the pins or use the spot-aim technique that is used by most experienced bowlers. In the spot-aim technique, your target out on the lane bed will be the second arrow, ten boards from the right side for right-handed bowlers, and the second arrow from the left for left-handers. Even more subtle choices in the spot aim are developed as the bowler becomes more and more advanced.

The Trial Swing. Take a trial swing as shown in figure 7. Remember that the trial swing is always made without moving the feet and without delivering the ball. From your stance position the ball will go out, down, back, and forward, and then return to the starting position. Have a firm grip on the ball so that it will not slip from your hand on the forward swing. Practice the trial swing until the pendulum of the arm is straight and smooth and without any hesitation.

7

6. A correct waist-high stance

7. The trial swing

8. Correcting the trial swing

It is important to let the weight of the ball carry it down and its momentum carry it into the backswing. Don't be tempted to force it down and back, or too cautious to let the ball swing freely. Too much caution will result in an attempt to carry the ball back to the backswing. Let the ball swing of its own weight through the downswing into the backswing, and from the top of the backswing forward. Your instructor may wish to assist you as shown in figure 8.

Figure 9 shows the instructor in a class situation. He checks the students individually as they take a trial swing to be sure that the ball fits properly, that the

9. Class taking a trial swing

fingers are in the appropriate holes, and that the ball is the proper weight. If the ball weighs too much, it pulls the shoulders down; a ball that is too light also causes problems. The instructor should check to see whether the swing is too fast or too hard, and whether the student is carrying the ball instead of swinging it like the pendulum of a clock. *Warning:* Beginners should not take the trial swing anywhere except on the approach facing the pins, as shown in figure 9. Then if the ball slips out of your hand because it does not fit properly or is too heavy, or because it is swung too hard, it can only go down the lane.

The One-Step Delivery

After you have practiced the trial swing, and the pendulum of the arm swing is straight and rhythmic without any hesitation, the *one-step delivery should be practiced* (figure 10). The one-step delivery is actually the last step of your complete approach and the delivery.

It is extremely important that you develop this phase so that it is smooth

10. The one-step delivery

(a)

(b)

and correct. It is in this last step that everything you have done in the entire approach must come together with perfect timing and coordination. Here you want to be *facing straight ahead*. There must be an exact *balance* and stability of the body, so that the weight of the ball and the natural momentum it has developed during a smooth arm swing will result in good leverage at the line (figure 10c). After the ball leaves the fingers, the arm should freely complete its pendulum swing in a full *follow-through* (figure 10d).

By practicing the one-step delivery it will help you to develop a sound and fluid delivery form. Practicing first without the ball as illustrated in figure 11 will make it easier and help to develop your concentration on the important things (figure 10): face straight ahead; knee slightly bent so that the body is stabilized and in balance as the ball is released; straight pendulum arm swing; and a full follow-through.

Practicing the one-step delivery (and all fundamentals) at home using a steam iron or other weighted object that has a handle will help considerably. Just remember to hang on to it!

After you have practiced without rolling the ball, and you feel that you can concentrate on the important points, practice the one-step delivery rolling the ball down the lane. Practice until you can incorporate all the important points men-

(c)

(d)

11. One-step delivery without the ball

12. One-step delivery with the ball

tioned above. Do not forget to use the correct stance position each time that you do the one-step delivery. These fundamentals will soon become automatic, and you will then be able to concentrate on the more advanced techniques.

Instructions for the One-Step Delivery

First: Note in figure 10a the bowler is in his normal stance position except that he is standing approximately 4 feet back of the foul line, with the entire weight on the right foot. (*Left-handed:* entire weight on the left foot.)

Second: *Without moving the feet,* swing the ball all the way back to the top of the backswing, as shown in figure 10b.

Third: Swing the ball forward easily and smoothly, simultaneously stepping forward with the left foot. *Don't force it. Notice the bowler does not lift the back foot off the approach;* he merely shifts his weight forward to the front foot. Most important, do not step too soon nor force the ball as you bring it forward.

Fourth: Let the arm continue all the way up to the side of the face and pose. If you can't pose for at least one second, you are not in balance, and the body is not stable at the foul line (figure 10d).

Remember to:

1. Bend the left knee (right for a left-hander) as in figure 10c and d;
2. Keep body slightly forward, figures 10c and d;
3. Follow through all the way up, figure 10d;
4. Keep the right foot (left for a left-hander) directly behind and in contact with the approach. Let the heel come up naturally, figures 10c and d.

It may help to count to yourself—*1, 2, 3;* or say to yourself—*down, back, forward.* This will help you to develop and feel the smooth, natural momentum of the ball and the free-swinging pendulum arm swing that is vital when you add the remaining steps of the approach.

Although you want to consistently train your arm in order to roll the ball on the ten board with the second arrow, as discussed on a previous page, do not be concerned if the ball drifts from that board while you are practicing the one-step delivery. That is not important at this time. If you happen to have your hand positioned for a hook delivery, the ball may roll across the lane into the opposite channel. Make no change or adjustment. It will be to your advantage later. Your concentration while practicing the one-step delivery must be on your timing, your balance, facing straight ahead, and following through at the foul line.

The one-step delivery is the best cure for correction of poor delivery form, side-wheeling, forcing the forward swing, poor hand (hook) position, not facing straight ahead, and many other approach and delivery problems discussed in chapter 3.

Figure 13 shows an instructor working on the one-step delivery with his class. In figure 13a, he has the entire group in tandem formation on the approach. Notice

(a) Without the ball

13. One-step delivery

(b) With the ball

that they are doing the one step *without* the ball and are under close observation; Figure 13b, the next operation, has one person on each lane taking the one step *with* the ball. This is their first attempt at rolling a ball down the lane. (The unison activity pictured here is definitely not recommended. It was done in this class merely to show that the entire group is doing it correctly.) Notice particularly the release and pose. Insisting on the pose now means a natural pose and perfect balance later.

Often the instructor finds it necessary to assist a pupil with the follow-through as shown in figure 14. The follow-through is one phase of instruction that cannot be overemphasized with the beginner, since many bowlers tend to neglect this fundamental as they become more experienced.

The Dry Run. The dry run, or trial run, coordinates the steps with the arm swing, from the starting position to the delivery position, but it is done *without* the ball (see figure 15).

It is helpful to practice the coordination and the timing of the arm-swing and the footwork through the use of the *dry run*. The dry run allows you to practice

14. Assisting with the following-through

all the fundamentals of the approach. You can practice at home with an iron or weighted object that you can grasp.

While practicing, do not run, poke along, or hesitate. On the last step (the slide step, figure 15), bend the knee slightly just as you did in the one-step delivery. Your steps and arm swing must be smooth and without hesitation. Repeat

15. The dry run

16. Instructor assisting in the dry run

the dry run until you can consistently maintain your balance and your body is firmly set (posed) at the foul line. As soon as you have coordinated this smooth pendulum swing with the three fast-walking steps described in the section on the three-step approach practice technique (p. 17), you will be ready to try it with the ball.

If you have problems with the dry run or with the three-step approach, your instructor may be able to help you by taking your right hand in his or her left hand and going to the foul line with you (see figure 16).

Instructors should note that the entire class can practice the dry run together as shown in figure 17. The courtesies of right-of-way on the lanes can be incorporated later.

The Three-Step Approach Practice Technique

Coordinating the *three-step approach* will not be difficult now that you have practiced with the one-step approach and delivery. The pendulum arm swing for the one-step delivery was a smooth and rhythmic *down-back-forward movement* (*1-2-3* if you used the counting technique).

This is exactly the timing to be used in the three-step approach (figure 18). In other words, for the right-handed bowler, the relatively fast walking steps of left-right-left are *timed to the down-back-forward (1-2-3) of the armswing!* For a

17. Class practicing the dry run

left-handed bowler, the steps are right-left-right timed to the armswing—down-back-forward (1-2-3).

Stance Position: Your stance position, which remains identical to that previously described, must be distant enough from the foul line to give you space to take the *three* steps. Generally, a tall person will position the feet approximately 1 foot in front of the 12-foot spots; a short person about 2 feet in front of those same spots.

Do not try to get leverage by tensing your arm and "muscling" the ball, or by forcefully raising up your body while you release the ball.

The fundamentals that you concentrated on in the one-step delivery are iden-

(a)

(b)

(c)

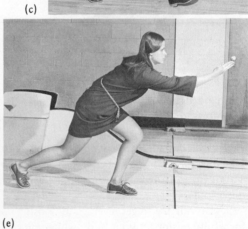

(d)

(e)

18. The three-step approach: The ball *must* be at the bottom of the
downswing (b) at the completion of the first step.

tical in the three-step approach. Continue to concentrate on and practice doing these correctly until your timing and coordination are perfect.

When these fundamentals have been done correctly, you will be able to feel the ball leave your fingers as you continue to follow through with your arm, as high as is comfortable in order to complete the full pendular arc of the arm swing (figure 19). During all this activity at the foul line, the body remains posed and balanced in order to give a stable base and full strength to the arm swing.

19. Follow-through and pose

20. Ball position on downswing

The key to the proper coordination of the feet and the arm swing (timing) in the three-step approach is bringing the ball down instantly when the first step is taken. The ball *must* be at the bottom of the down-swing at the completion of the first step (see figure 20).

Your instructor will want to watch you in order to assess what phase of your game most needs attention. Proper approach, timing, and coordination are the first concerns, followed by proper delivery form. Your teacher will point out faults that should be corrected. Some faults are forcing the forward swing, losing balance during the delivery, twisting the arm during the pendulum swing, a crooked approach, or a poor rolling ball. When your instructor mentions a particular fault, refer to the corrections section (chapter 3) of this manual to further assist in making the appropriate adjustments.

As in all sports, to perfect the style that feels best and gives you good scores, it takes a lot of practice. Those who wish to consistently get high scores must be willing to take the time to practice these fundamentals. Be sure, also, that you are practicing the fundamentals correctly so that poor habits will not become a part of your bowling style.

You are now ready to deliver the ball. Did you charge to the foul line? Many beginners tend to go too fast. Make your approach rhythmic and smooth. Let the weight of the ball do the work of swinging your arm. Do not "muscle" the ball in the forward swing as the last step is taken.

It is possible that you will roll some of the first few balls into the left channel. Beginners have a tendency to pull the arm across in front of the body as they release the ball. This is called *pointing* the ball. A great improvement can be made by releasing the ball beyond the foul line and following through with your arm straight out on a line to the second arrow. Accuracy will come with practice and after mastery of a smooth, fluid arm swing and coordinated footwork. This coordination of footwork with the arm swing in a smooth approach, and the essentials of an acceptable delivery of the ball at the foul line, should be uppermost in your mind.

You do not need to be concerned at this point with perfecting the hand position for a hook or a straight ball, or for the other advanced techniques. There are special sections later in this book that will cover these topics. First you must master the fundamentals needed to become a skilled bowler.

Reread these first sections on the fundamentals when you are having trouble with your approach and delivery technique, or if your instructor has not yet had an opportunity to work with you. Review of the fundamentals is preferable to practicing unwanted habits that will be hard to change later.

Your instructor may want to make some changes in your starting (stance) position in order to increase your accuracy. However, these changes should be only *slight* from those recommended here. A very small change, such as 1 inch (the width of one board), will make a tremendous change in how accurately the ball will contact the pins 60 feet down the lane! If you develop a natural hook and are right-handed, for example, your ball may miss the pins by going by them on the left, although you have hit your target spot squarely. In this case you should move your starting position to the left a bit (see figure 29). Or if you roll a straight ball, you may find that straddling the fifteen board and hitting the second arrow will not hit the head pin. To remedy this, move your starting position slightly to adjust the angle. Left-handed bowlers use these same relative adjustments on their left side of the lane.

One special bit of advice: Some students tend to throw the ball instead of rolling it. Do not force the forward swing for extra speed. Let the ball come through the forward swing and develop its momentum naturally. Remember: *Roll the ball, don't throw it.*

Notice in figure 21 the fine delivery form displayed by a class that was taught using the three-step method. All students show perfect balance, are facing straight ahead, and were able to release the ball and pose for the photo of the follow-through—in spite of the distraction of bowling for the camera. A person learning to bowl on his or her own will use the same procedure step by step.

2. THE COMPLETE APPROACH AND DELIVERY

Changing from the Three-Step to the Four-Step Approach

You should now have developed good basic technique. You should be facing straight ahead, have good balance, and a straight pendulum arm swing as you release the ball. The proper hand position will be discussed later.

21. Good delivery form

At this time, you must decide whether you can improve your timing and coordination further by adding another step to your footwork as described in the section on the four-step approach, p. 26.

You will need to experiment with the additional step or steps to determine whether or not it feels more natural. If an additional step or steps feels more comfortable and natural, be sure that it does not negatively change or interfere with your timing, coordination, facing straight ahead, and being able to be in balance and posed at the foul line as you release the ball and follow through.

Is a change from three-step technique to the full four-step approach really necessary? For years the three-step approach, although used by some great bowlers, was frowned upon. In order to be considered a top performer, a good bowler simply had to employ a four- or five-step approach. Unfortunately, we have no statistics to defend a position on the number of steps in the best approach; thus the entire matter becomes an issue of individual preference. The main goal is to keep the pendulum swing smooth and to coordinate the footwork, regardless of the number of steps taken, with the natural rhythm and momentum of that arm swing.

We recommend the four-step approach for most bowlers. It generally fits the rhythm of the arm-swing pattern that is composed of the four parts of *out-down-back-forward* in the full approach. That is the push-away, the downswing, the backswing, and the forward swing in the full pendular arc of the arm swing.

Those who need added ball speed should definitely make the change to the four-step approach. The extra step and the push-away from the chin-high position increases ball speed and approach momentum (see figure 22).

22. Changing from a three- to a four-step approach

23. Four-step approach

(a) Stance

(b) Push-away

Four-Step Approach

The change from the three-step to the *four-step approach* is quite simple. Take your usual starting position, then step straight back on the runway about 18 inches to make room for the extra step. Now take your regular approach, but (1) carry the ball or slightly extend it straight forward as you take one small, first step before starting the downswing of the ball. (Start this first small step with the opposite foot from the one that you started with in the three-step approach as in figure 22). (2) Now complete the approach and ball delivery just as you practiced in the three-step approach and delivery technique (see figures 23 and 24).

You will likely find that you will make these changes correctly on the very first try, since you will make no change in your arm-swing rhythm. The only changes are that you carry or move the ball slightly forward through the additional first small step before it starts the downswing, and you start the first step with the other foot.

(c) Release

(d) Pose

24. Assisting the push-away

To explain further, the right-handed bowler will take the first small step with the right foot as the ball is carried forward, followed by the downswing of the ball as the second step is taken. Then as the ball continues in the backswing and the forward swing, the third step and the final slide step blend with the rhythm of the arm-swing. The left-handed bowler will follow this same coordination except that the first-step is initiated with the left foot.

As you practice, you will develop a slight push-away of the ball from its position near or slightly above your waist. It will become automatic with practice. This is exactly what you want to do; coordinate the first step with this slight push-away to get the ball in motion.

If you have difficulty in remembering to start with the correct foot, right-handed bowlers should raise the right heel off the runway and shift the weight

25. The coordination of the swing and the four-step approach

(a) Stance

(b) Push-away

(c) Downswing

to the left foot in the stance position. Left-handed bowlers should raise the left heel off the runway and shift the weight to the right foot. This will remind you to step off on the correct foot.

Figure 25 shows a very skilled bowler in the stance, the push-away, down-swing, backswing, forward swing, release of the ball, and finally, a full follow-through.

Figures 23a and 23b show the class making the change from the three-step to the four-step approach. Notice that the entire class automatically pushes the ball out in front of the body on the first step, even though they are told to carry it. This push-away is, of course, what should be done, but the concept of carrying the ball lets each beginner develop the push-away instinctively, rather than having to think "step and push" while learning.

(d) Backswing

(e) Forward swing
and delivery

(f) Follow-through

Figures 23c and 23d show the fine finished product. Without question, learning to bowl using this method practically ensures a good approach and ball-delivery form. In some cases, the beginner will bring the ball down too soon in the push-away instead of out in front only. In this case, the instructor can assist by guiding the arm forward, as shown in figure 24.

Analysis of the Four-Step Approach

Stance. When you assume your stance position (figure 25a, take a firm, comfortable grip on the ball, with both hands under it. Hold the ball slightly to the right of the center of the body; let the left hand do most of the work of supporting the ball. The positions of the index and little fingers have little to do with the grip. They may be close in or spread out, whichever is comfortable. The feet should be together, and the elbows should be close to your sides.

Push-Away. The push-away (figures 25b) is the take-off in the approach. Before you start the push-away, shift your weight to your left foot (the foot that stays in place when you step off with the other foot), so that the first step can be taken with the right foot, smoothly and without lurching forward. With the start of the first step, start the ball forward and push it out to the *full arm's length* (figure 25b) with the first step. Be careful, however, not to push the ball out too far, which would cause too long a first step and possibly a delay in the arm swing. These two movements—push-away and first step—must be made together for a good four-step approach.

Second Step. On the second step of the approach, the ball moves from the end of the *push-away* to the bottom of the arc of the downswing. The left foot completes the second step at the same time that the ball reaches the bottom of the arc (figure 25c).

Third Step. As the third step is completed, the ball should reach the top of the backswing, approximately at shoulder height (figure 25d). The right shoulder is the pivot point for the pendulum, and the pendulum swing must be in a straight line over the ball's intended path. There is no prescribed position for the left arm during the approach. Use it naturally for balance.

Fourth Step. On the fourth step, the slide step, the ball and the left foot will start forward at the same time if your timing has been good (figure 25e). If your timing is not correct, the left foot (slide foot) will get to the foul line before the ball is in position to be delivered out onto the lane. When you get "out of time" this way, you will force the speed of the forward swing in an effort to "catch up." This will generally cause the ball to drop in back of the foul line. The black marks you may often see on the approach in back of the foul line are made when the ball is dropped in this way.

The most overworked phrases in bowling—"Pitch the ball out"; "You're dropping the ball"; and "You're forcing the ball"—all imply the same thing: the approach is not properly coordinated and the slide foot is consequently arriving at the foul line before the ball. Incidentally, the length of the slide is immaterial.

It will vary depending on the approach speed, the bowler's height and weight, and so on. The bowler illustrated has a long, smooth slide as shown in figure 25f. Although many bowlers depend on the slide to bring the body to a smooth stop, some bowlers have no perceptible slide at all. Their style enables them to maintain balance during the delivery without one. Proper balance with the body firmly set (posed) during the delivery is the important consideration, not the length of the slide.

Walking Straight. To develop accuracy and form, take your steps to the foul line along a straight line and face straight ahead during delivery of the ball. Check the board on which your forward foot is planted at the foul line after you have delivered the ball. Did you drift to the right or left of the board used at your starting position? It will be too late to correct the delivery just made, but if you check for drifting to either side you can work to avoid repeating this error. *Develop the habit of noting your finishing position at the foul line.*

Students will now have some idea of how to approach the foul line and deliver the ball by developing a degree of mastery of the basic principles outlined in the previous section or by prior experience. The skills of a coordinated approach and delivery are fundamental to learning and applying the finer points of the game. Therefore, all bowlers, regardless of present experience or proficiency, should have a working knowledge of the instructional methods introduced in this section and developed more fully in the next section.

Nearly all of today's bowling champions use a four- or five-step approach. Five steps are not generally recommended, especially for the beginner. The instructor can observe and determine the proper number of steps required for the bowler to achieve a smooth and consistent approach and delivery. The four-step approach is by far the most popular, and nearly all bowlers can master it.

3. SPOT, PIN, AND LINE BOWLING

The most common methods of aiming are known as spot bowling, pin bowling, and line bowling. Is it better to look and aim at a spot on the lane, or is it better to aim directly at the pins? The answer is not the same for every student. Ninety-nine out of a hundred bowling champions aim at a spot on the lane. We prefer spot bowling and recommend that all students adopt this system. The majority of beginners will find spot bowling the easier method to master if they give it a fair trial. It is easier to hit a target 16 feet away than one 60 feet away. True, a miss of 1 inch at the target spot can mean a miss of 5 or 6 inches at the pins, but it is still easier to hit the nearer target.

The spot bowler aims at a spot on the lane, not at the pins. For the beginner, the second arrow from the right is usually the target. The bowler concentrates on rolling the center of the ball over this spot, and if he or she delivers the ball consistently and hits this spot, the ball will hit the pins in the same place every time.

Many spot bowlers prefer aiming at the spots that are 8 feet in front of the foul line. They find this closer target easier to hit. However, beginners who try this method of aiming should be aware of its shortcomings. It may cause dumping of the ball, instead of lifting it, and cutting the follow through instead of reaching out and up.

The pin bowler aims directly at the pins. In a sense, this is aiming by instinct. Nevertheless the ball must still follow the line that the delivery pendulum gives it. Drifting—walking to the left in the approach—is more of a problem for the pin bowler than it is for the spot bowler. Pin bowlers who stand right of center on the approach in order to get the maximum angle into the pocket, invariably drift to the left. The spot bowler, on the other hand, because his or her arm swing is on a direct line with the target, is able to walk in a straighter line towards the target.

The line bowler visualizes a line over which he or she wants the ball to travel. The bowler then picks two or three check points on this line (designated by a "C" in figure 26) and concentrates on rolling the ball over the check points.

You may adopt whichever method you wish. However, no matter how you aim—at a spot or directly at the pins—as a beginner you should still try to roll the ball over the second arrow for a strike.

Generally speaking, you have been straddling the fifteen board in the stance position, and you have been rolling the ball over the second arrow to hit the strike pocket. The fifteenth board contains the second dot from the right. This stance

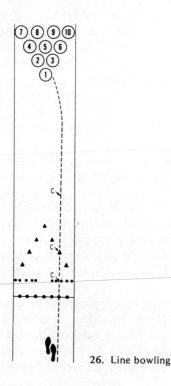

26. Line bowling

position is used under normal conditions by most bowlers who have an average hook.

If your ball is hooking too much to hit the strike pocket, move your starting location a board or two in to the left. *You will still aim at the second arrow.* If the lane is fast (see chapter 4, section 18, Lane Conditions) and the ball is not coming up to the pocket, the opposite adjustment must be made. Move your starting location out to the right a board or two, but continue to roll the ball over the second arrow.

Many spot bowlers find it difficult to roll the center of the ball exactly over a narrow spot. When they try to put the ball over a certain board or arrow, they stiffen up and lose the proper roll of the ball. In this case *area bowling* is a better method. Instead of trying to pinpoint the ball over a single arrow or board, make your target an area of two or three boards. This method works well not just for beginners; several top bowlers use this system of aiming.

Many experienced bowlers find it easier to pick a different target on the lane than to change their starting position; but this method is usually less successful for beginners. If when the ball rolls over the second arrow it hooks too much, the experienced bowler may aim one or two boards outside of the second arrow. This system has the advantage of keeping the body square with the foul line. You may be one of the rare beginning bowlers who develop a wide, sweeping hook ball, in which case you will profit more by changing your target than by moving your starting position far enough to the left to compensate for the wide hook.

The Foul Line

The foul line separates the approach runway from the lane. It is against the rules to touch *anything* beyond the foul line. A foul is usually committed by the toe of the shoe going past the foul line as the ball is delivered. It is also a foul if the hand touches the wall or anything else past the line. In the beginning, don't worry about stepping or sliding over the line; concentrate on form and timing. Learning to stay back of the foul line will come later.

The Ball's Path to the Pins

A bowling ball may take three possible paths down the lane: (1) the right-to-left curve—of which the *hook ball* is the best example; (2) the "no curve"—the *straight ball;* and (3) the left-to-right curve—the *back-up* and the *reverse hook.* (These names are applied to curves thrown by right-handers.)

All bowlers should learn to roll the hook ball (figure 27), if possible, although mastery of the straight ball can be effective for those lacking the necessary strength for the hook ball. Do not develop the back-up and reverse hook, because they are ineffective. The *curve,* of which you may have heard, is merely an exaggerated ineffective hook.

27. A very good hook

4. PLAYING SPARES

The Three Basic Spare Angles

If all ten pins are knocked down by the first roll in a frame, a *strike* is scored. If the first roll leaves one or more pins standing, the rules allow a second roll—just one chance—to knock down the remaining pins. The pins that remain standing after the first roll are referred to as a *leave*. Knocking down the leave scores a *spare;* bowlers say that the spare is *converted*.

Good spare shooting is the foundation of top bowling. Should you miss a spare, it will generally take three strikes in a row, a *turkey,* to gain ground on the bowler who is getting good counts and converting spares.

Three basic aiming angles are used to convert spares. These are center-to-center, left-to-right, and right-to-left. The first, the strike position, is a center-to-center angle (see figure 29). Leaves of the 4-pin, the 7-pin, or both, are played from right to left (see figures 29b and 29d). Leaves on the right side of the lane, such as the 6-pin or the 10-pin, are played from the left-to-right angle (figures 29c and 28). This principle applies whether the bowler is right- or left-handed.

To convert the 10-pin, all right-handed bowlers who roll a hook (or curve) ball should aim at the third arrow from the right. If they roll a straight ball (no hook or curve), they should position their feet on the same board, but aim at the center or fourth arrow (see figure 29c). To convert the 7-pin, they should aim

(a) Starting position is the left side of the approach

(b) Note where left foot finishes. This is important

28. Hook ball: playing the 10-pin

(c) The ball's path is from the left to the right

29. Basic spare angles

(a) Center-to-center   (b) Right-to-left   (c) Left-to-right   (d) Right-to-left

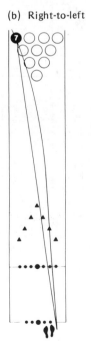

somewhere between the second and third arrows from the right (figure 29b), depending on the amount of the hook. (Left-handers count the arrows from the left, of course.) Figure 29d shows the conversion of the 2-4-7 pin spare by the right-handed hook and straight ball. A mirrored image will give the left-hander's targets for the relatively same left and right side of the lane angles. However, the pin numbers will not be accurate and must be reversed.

The illustrations in figure 29 show that the ball passes over the second or third arrow or somewhere in between them in all three basic spare angles. Thus the second and third arrows are the only targets a bowler needs. Changing the location of the stance position makes all other necessary adjustments.

The professional bowler who rolls the ball inside, to the left of the center arrow, or outside, to the right of the first arrow, is making an extremely delicate adjustment, seeking the maximum benefit of an angle he or she feels is best for the lane conditions at hand. Such fine adjustments are matters of individual expert style.

As a rule, a leave that includes the 1- and 5-pins should be converted from the center-to-center angle. All other spares that include the head pin, a few of which are illustrated in figure 30, should be played from the left or right. First assume the strike position, then move the feet a board or two in or out according to what other pins are left with the head pin and the amount of hook on the ball.

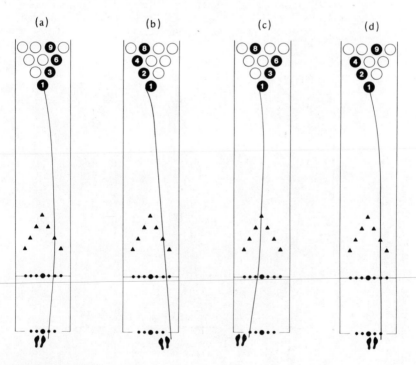

30. Head pin leaves

An exception to this rule is the 1-3-6-8 leave illustrated in figure 30c. This is a common leave for beginners. Increase your chances of converting this difficult spare by playing over the center arrow.

There are so many different combinations of pins that can be left after the first roll that it is impossible to list them all here. That is why we suggest the three basic spare angles explained in this section.

Figure 31 illustrates the conversion of the 2-4 spare. Imagine the line that will be the intended path of the ball. This line will go from the outside edge of the right shoe to the spot you wish the ball to hit. If you are a spot bowler, move a bit on the approach until this line crosses a convenient target—usually the second or third arrow. This imaginary line is similar to sighting a gun—the rear sight is the spot at the foul line over which you intend to roll the ball, the front sight is the target arrow on the lane. The pin bowler will use the same method, only his target in this case will be the 2-pin. It makes no difference how much hook, if any, the bowler rolls. The above system will work provided the imaginary line the bowler draws corresponds with the exact amount of hook he or she rolls.

Therefore, straight ball or hook, the principle is the same. You line up your sights, walk in a straight line *parallel with this line,* and roll the ball over this imaginary line and over the target.

Figure 32 shows the proper method of playing the 5-9 spare. The more left-to-right angle a bowler can play on this spare, the less chance there is of chopping

31. Converting the 2-4 spare

32. Converting the 5-9 spare

the front pin off the back pin *(picking a cherry)*. This same principle, of course, also applies to other spares where a chop of the front pin is a distinct possibility, such as the 6-10, 2-5, 3-6, and so on.

As a point of information for the novice, if, for example, you are trying to convert a corner pin for a spare, and your ball drops into the channel in front of the pin, but the wobble of the ball in the channel hits the pin, it is *not* a spare. Once the ball has left the lane surface, any pins it knocks down *do not* count.

5. BOWLING ETIQUETTE

Rules of etiquette are as much a part of bowling as knocking down the pins. They are only common-sense practices, but we may sometimes forget these little things. Here are some bowling courtesies:

1. When you check your coat, also check your temper.
2. Watch the bowlers on your left and right. The first person who is ready to bowl must be allowed the courtesy of delivering the ball first. Two bowlers on adjoining lanes are *never* to start their approaches at the same time. This is an important rule everywhere.
3. Do not pick up your ball when the bowler on the adjoining lane is ready to bowl. If you do, it will interrupt his or her concentration.
4. Return to the head of the runway when you have delivered the ball. Do not stand at the foul line waiting for the ball to be returned. Remember, the bowler on the adjoining lane is waiting for you to finish your delivery.
5. Always be ready to bowl when it is your turn.
6. Confine your "body English" to your own lane. It not only distracts bowlers on the adjoining lanes; it could result in an accident.
7. Do not bring food or drinks into the bowlers' section. A spilled drink could cause an injury or a foul.
8. Remember, splits, misses, and taps are part of the game, so don't get upset when you come up against them.
9. Return your rental bowling shoes to the desk, and return the house bowling ball to its proper spot in the storage rack.

An exception to bowling courtesy has to be made when an instructor and student bowler are working or the entire class is doing a drill simultaneously on the runway. The bowlers nearby must try to ignore them.

II

THE MECHANICS
OF BOWLING

6. TIMING

The first chapter of this manual briefly discussed the fundamentals for the beginner and the suggested class procedures for the instructor. In this chapter, the key
fundamentals—timing, delivery form, and arm and hand position (in that order)—
are explained and emphasized in detail. Chapter 3, "Faults and Corrections," will
show the "before" and "after" of just about every possible bowling problem. The
methods outlined are not only intended to get the beginner off to a skillful start,
but also to provide a reference for the experienced bowler in order to correct flaws
that may develop at any stage of the game.

Timing in the Approach

*Timing in the approach is fitting the steps, or footwork, to the swing of the
bowling ball (pendulum arm swing).* The bowling ball must move like a free-swinging pendulum, smoothly and without hesitation or break in the rhythm of *out-
down-back-forward* movement.

The ball should not be forced or "muscled" through any part of the arm
swing and the delivery. If force is applied, it works against the natural momentum
and forces that the weight of the ball will generate during the arm swing, especially
during the release.

The shoulder joint is the pivot point from which the arm swings. It is extremely important that the wrist be kept straight and firm throughout the entire
approach, delivery, and follow-through. This is referred to as a "locked wrist." You
can visualize that the arm, swinging freely from the shoulder joint, acts as a long
lever with the bowling ball at the end.

In bowling the feet must stay in time with the swing of the ball. Thus the feet must get the body to the foul line at the precise instant that will most effectively transfer all forward momentum into the release of the ball.

When the timing is correct, the last step of the approach and the slight bend of the knee of that leg bring the body to a stopped and balanced position. There is no hop at the foul line, no lifting or turning of the body. It remains set and still in a posed position, as the arm swings the ball and releases it out over the foul line. Thus the forces generated by the momentum of the unforced and unhesitating ball swing, added to that of the body moving forward in time to that arm swing, can be transferred into the release as the body comes to a firm and posed stop at the foul line.

While the four-step approach is rhythmically more suited to the four-part movement pattern (out-down-back-forward) of the arm swinging the ball, the number of steps used is not the most important consideration.

If you do not already have a pendulum arm swing and footwork that gives you good timing, practice methods such as the trial swing, the one-step delivery, and the dry run can help perfect your technique and timing (see chapter 3).

Comparison of Styles

The Four-Step Approach. Compare the push-away (start) of the bowler in figure 25 with the bowler in figure 33. Notice the difference in the *stance position* and the *push-a-way*, yet both have flawless timing. The bowler in figure 33 is more comfortable stooping over and pushing the ball up as he takes his first step.

33. One style of push-away and delivery in the four-step approach

(b) Push-away

(a) Stance

(c) Downswing

(d) Backswing

(e) Forward swing

(f) Delivery

(g) Follow-through

Incidentally, this bowler has the bent elbow "à la Don Carter." It is not recommended. However, it does not affect his bowling, and Don Carter will go down in history as one of the greatest ever.

Fitting the steps to the natural pendulum swing couldn't be emphasized more than it is with the bowler in figure 34, who is Eddie Hansen, one of the best bowlers in the northwest. He simply feels more comfortable taking the extremely short steps, except for the LAST step. There is very little difference between his last step and that of any other bowler. We certainly do NOT recommend anyone emulate this style. It does, however, emphasize the point that the steps are fit to the swing, NOT the swing to the steps.

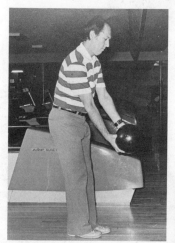

34. Fitting the steps to the armswing (timing)

Notice how short the first three steps are.

Question: "Where should the ball be in the push-away and the downswing?"
The answer varies somewhat with the bowler.

Compare the bowler in figure 25 with the bowlers in figures 35 and 36. What would happen to the smooth pendulum swings of these bowlers if they tried another style? So many bowlers get fouled up when they are told that they must push the ball out a certain way and a certain distance.

35. Smooth arm swing

(a) Stance

(b) Push-away

(c) Downswing

(d) Backswing

(e) Forward swing and delivery

(f) Follow-through

(a) Stance

(b) Push-away and downswing

36. Another smooth four-stepper

(c) and (d) Backswing

(e) and (f) Forward swing and release

(g) Follow-through

Generally, when a bowler appears to be rushing the last two steps, it's the result of a faulty push-away, which is the cause of a "three-step swing and a four-step approach." A good example of this is shown in chapter three, figures 77a and 78, pp. 89 and 91.

You need only observe the pros on television to see a variety of styles. Notice particularly how they vary in the push-away and the distance the ball travels during the first two steps.

Should the push-away go *straight out?* The majority will. However, many will go beyond this point, as the bowler in figure 36 demonstrates. Another smooth four-stepper, he swings the ball to the bottom of the arc as he takes his first step. He does not rush, there is no hitch whatsoever in his smooth walk to the line. Several top bowlers use this style. The key is, fit the steps to the natural swing.

At this point, we would like to mention the many bowlers who have excellent qualities and a four-step approach, yet, because the vast majority of pros use five steps, these four-steppers change to five steps. We don't like to see this change made. The four-stepper gets the ball to the top of the backswing naturally and high enough to give the ball the needed speed, so why add a fifth step? The bowler in figure 35 takes three steps to get the ball to the top of the backswing and has a smooth four-step approach, so, again, a fifth step is not really needed.

The Five-Step Approach. Which *approach* will give a bowler the best timing— the three-step, the four-step, or the five-step approach? The answer is *any one of them.* Although the majority of pros use a five-step approach, the three-and the four-step approach can be just as good.

Figures 37, 38, and 39 show the excellent stroke of five-step bowlers. Notice the smooth, free-swinging pendulum. There is no hitch and no forcing at any point

37. A five-step approach

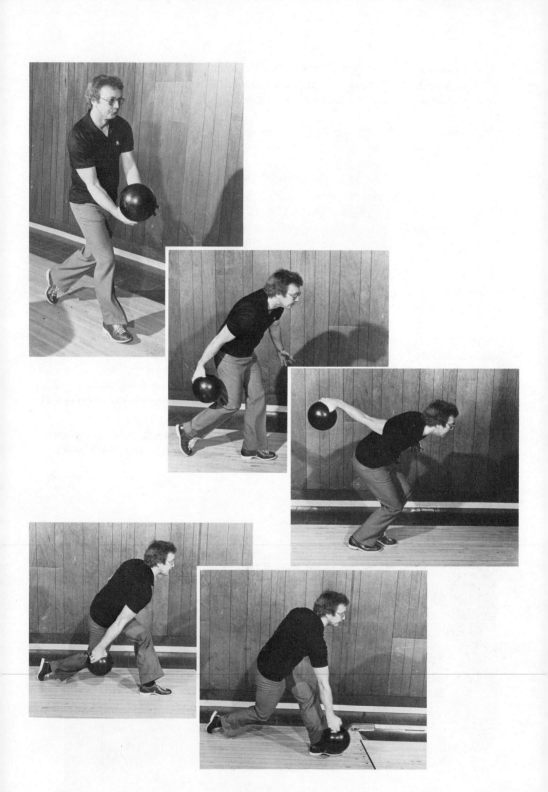

38. Another five-step approach, showing a slight variation in the stance and push-away, otherwise just as good

39. Another variation in the stance and push-away, also showing excellent timing and stroke

in the swing. Notice that the right shoulder, the pivot point of the pendulum swing, remains directly over the intended path of the ball. This bowler's smooth approach shows the importance of *fitting the steps to the natural swing.*

As with the four-step approach, it is not critical where the ball is on a particular step.

The Three-Step Approach. The sequence illustrated in figure 40 shows the smooth pendulum swing and three-step approach of the skilled bowler who has a high average. For years the three-step approach, although used by some great bowlers, has been frowned upon. However, there are no statistics to defend a position for or against the number of steps employed in the ideal approach. Thus, the matter becomes one of individual preference.

We do recommend the four-step approach for the three-step bowler who needs *added ball speed.* The higher stance position with the higher push-away simply generates more power.

Obviously, we do not consider a three-step approach a fault. If a bowler feels comfortable taking three steps, has a smooth swing, good balance, leverage and follow-through, and excellent ball roll, why should he or she change just because the majority of bowlers prefer four or five steps?

40. A three-step approach

7. THREE FUNDAMENTALS
FOR DEVELOPING GOOD DELIVERY FORM

Delivery form and style are affected by many factors—a bowler's size and strength, natural coordination, the speed of the swing, and the length of his or her steps. Nevertheless, every student can develop good delivery form by practicing these three fundamentals: (1) face straight ahead as you deliver the ball and as you follow through; (2) be in balance for good leverage as you complete the slide and delivery at the foul line; and (3) swing your arm in a straight pendulum and follow through directly to your target.

Figure 41 shows four bowlers, each with a different delivery style. Each of these styles is correct, however, because each exhibits the three fundamentals perfectly. Bear in mind that the right shoulder joint is the pivot point for the pendulum swing and that the arm must be able to swing straight and easily over the intended path of the ball. Turning the shoulders and the hips away from parallel to the foul line will hurt your accuracy. Observe the three basic rules of a good delivery while you develop your own style.

41. Left-handed, right-handed, women, or men:
the fundamentals are the same

When you practice the fundamentals, "pose" at the foul line after you deliver the ball to develop stability and balance. Training yourself to pose at the foul line will eliminate many faults. Try to keep the back foot on the approach directly behind the body during the delivery. This will help you hold your shoulders and hips parallel to the foul line. As long as you can keep your shoulders and hips parallel to the foul line, you can throw the back leg to the side for balance if that is more natural for you. The most important single feature of a good delivery is the bent forward knee that supports the body weight. Your delivery form is good if you can look straight down over your front knee and see your toes pointed straight ahead.

Facing Straight Ahead

With your shoulders and hips parallel to the foul line, you will face straight ahead more easily if you bend your forward knee and shift your weight to your forward leg. The slide foot should, of course, point straight down the lane during the delivery. Some bowlers find that keeping the back foot on the approach, as shown in figure 42, will help guide the body to face straight ahead. Many bowlers,

42. Facing straight ahead

however, have to throw the back leg around to the side for balance. It is not essential to keep the back foot on the approach. The important thing is to keep the shoulders and hips perpendicular to the line of flight of the ball. However, we recommend that beginners make every attempt to keep the back foot directly behind and on the approach (figure 42).

Balance and Leverage

Balance. Deliver the ball in perfect balance, as if you were posing for a picture like figure 43.

Figure 44 shows another bowler with good balance and leverage. The trunk of the body is held upright and parallel to the foul line; the forward foot is pointed straight ahead.

43. Perfect balance

44. Another example of good balance and leverage

45. Fair balance and leverage

46. An example of poor leverage

47. Another example of less-than-perfect leverage

The bowler in figure 45 has fair balance and leverage. However, accuracy due to his "dip and turn" will be inconsistent. Chapter 3, which deals with faults and corrections, shows the same bowler after the correction was made in figure 105, p. 118.

The bowlers in figures 46 and 47 have good balance at the line, but poor leverage. Both were corrected by simply having them move closer to the line and slow down the speed of the steps. Remember that the approach is a *fast walk,* not a run.

48. Squaring the shoulders with the foul line

The bowler in figure 48 bends forward, very low, and is swinging his right leg in the air. The important thing is this: he is facing square with the foul line. Therefore this is an acceptable delivery, because it is natural for him to bend in this manner as he delivers the ball, and he is strong enough to have sufficient ball-release lift and power. Many bowlers would not be able to generate power with this style.

If you crank the ball (excessive turn and lift), as the bowler in figure 49 is doing, the knee bend, vertical body position, and the shoulder lined up with the target become critical. You could not be very accurate if your delivery form were, for example, like the bowler shown in figure 45.

49. Cranking the ball

50. Straight swing and follow-through

Straight Pendulum Swing
and Follow-Through

Straight pendulum arm swing and follow-through are shown in figure 50. The motion of your arm during the approach should be a smooth pendulum swing— out, down, back, forward, and follow-through. From the end of the push-away, gravity pulls the ball down and inertia moves it into the backswing. It is not necessary to strain to reach the top of the backswing. Gravity and inertia again bring the ball down and forward to the point of release *without forcing*. Guard against variations in your pendulum swing. Any variation from a perfectly straight pendulum swing increases the chance of missing your target.

The Follow-Through. The follow-through is as important to a bowler as it is to a golfer or a baseball pitcher. A successful bowler must deliver the ball out past the foul line with the arm continuing on through to complete the swing and follow-through. Do not swing the ball out from the body to the right or to the left across the front of the body. Keep the pendulum arm swing straight and follow through toward the target, as in figure 50. End the pendulum swing with your arm to the side of your head. This will help eliminate the problem of pulling the ball across its intended line of flight. Develop a good follow-through early; it will be a tremendous asset.

If you roll a hook ball, the follow-through encourages the hook lift by the fingers. The straight-ahead follow-through will greatly assist the development of accurate control. The follow-through completes the excellent delivery form of the bowler in figure 50.

To summarize delivery form, figure 51 shows what it's all about. No matter what angle or line you are playing, straight down the ten board as shown in figure 50, swinging the ball four boards as shown in figure 51, or playing the tight line as shown in figure 63, the better bowler will be the one who can most consistently place the ball on *both* targets, the board beyond the foul line and the target at the arrows. (This is the same technique.as in shooting a rifle, using the front sight and the rear sight).

Many champion bowlers have unorthodox styles. They realize their faults better than anyone else, but through constant practice they have integrated these faults into their style so successfully that they can deliver the ball the same way every time. *Consistency* is the key to better bowling. It is far easier, however, to develop and maintain consistency with an easy, smooth, graceful approach and a delivery that does not contain basic flaws. If stars with unorthodox styles were to give you any tips, they would insist that you learn to bowl the easy and comfortable way—the correct way.

Hand Position

There are two hand positions that are recommended and that are the most effective. These are the *hook-ball* delivery and the *straight-ball* delivery positions. We will refer to them also as hand *delivery* positions because it is obviously at the exact moment of delivery of the ball that it is essential to employ one of these hand positions.

Between the two, the hook-ball delivery is the most effective. The exception is the bowler who does not have the wrist strength to maintain the hand position for the hook delivery throughout the stance, approach and arm swing, and the delivery. In that case, the straight-ball delivery should be used.

The *back-up* ball or the *reverse-hook* hand positions should be avoided. These deliveries are created when the wrist and hand rotate outward away from the body as the release of the ball occurs. These deliveries are weak since the power of the ball has essentially dissipated by the time it contacts the pins, because the spin

51. A summary of good delivery form

(revolutions) on the ball is moving away from, rather than into, the pins. Thus greater deflection rather than drive into the pins is produced. On occasion a bowler may be fairly successful with the hand position for the back-up ball or reverse-hook (see figure 129, p. 146), but it is rare.

Straight-Ball Hand Position. The straight ball rolls end-over-end, straight toward the target (point of aim). The hand position of the straight ball is simply having the palm of the hand directly underneath and behind the ball not only during the stance position, but throughout the entire approach and the release.

This hand position is described as one in which the thumb is pointed to 12 o'clock and the middle and ring fingers are at 6 o'clock. As the ball leaves the fingers when they are in this 6 o'clock position, it will roll end-over-end in a straight path with no sideward spin. Thus it has only the force of the forward roll acting on the pins.

Hook-Ball Hand Position. The hook ball has a forward force equal to that of the straight ball as it enters the triangle or group of pins. It has a powerful additional force created by its sideward spin which is turning the ball into the pins.

The weight of the pins reacting against the ball as it makes contact will cause the ball to deflect regardless of the hand position. However, a good hook-ball that creates the dual forces just described counteracts this deflection more effectively than other delivery forms. With the mixing action of the hook, the ball very powerfully continues to drive through to create optimal pin-mixing action.

The correct hand position for the hook ball is extremely important. The most effective and accurate position for the *right-handed* bowler is that in which the thumb is pointed at 10 o'clock and the middle and ring fingers are within the 4 and 5:30 o'clock range. For the *left-handed* bowler, the thumb is pointed at 1 o'clock, and the bowling fingers are between 6:30 and 8 o'clock.

Observe the firm wrist and fingertips in the approach and delivery form of all the better bowlers shown in this text. Each of these bowlers has unique characteristics and style. However, certain fundamental elements remain the same among all of them, such as the firm wrist, firm fingertips as the ball is released out over the foul line, approach and delivery timing, and arm swing and follow-through toward the intended target.

8. ANALYSIS OF THE HOOK BALL

All top bowlers roll a hook ball. Why? Because it will get more strikes. Figure 52 shows the 10-pin triangle and the ball. The ball is rolled into the 1-3 pocket; then it hits between the 5- and 9-pins so that the 5-pin can take out the 8. This is the

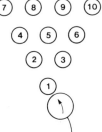

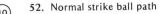
52. Normal strike ball path

53. Normal pattern

normal strike pattern. If the ball is to be effective, contact with the head pin must deflect it as little as possible from this normal path.

Applying a spin to the ball as it is released causes it to curve into the pins. The inertia from the sideward force of the curve offsets the tendency of the ball to deflect after striking the head pin; the ball digs in and drives into the 5-pin. In the normal strike pattern the ball must hit the 5-pin, which is therefore called the *king pin*. Since the 5-pin is directly behind the head pin, the ball may miss the 5-pin if if deflects after hitting the 1–3 pocket. Remember that the ball is rolling like a wheel, not spinning like a top.

The hook ball gives the bowler a "bigger" pocket; that is, the ball need not always hit the exact center of the 1–3 pocket to be effective, because the right-to-left drive of the ball into the pins affords a much higher probability of hitting the 5-pin. The "high" hits (those closer to the head pin) and the "thin" hits (those closer to the 3-pin) have a better chance of striking with a good hook ball. Figure 53 shows the normal strike pattern. Notice that there are three different pin spreads:

1. Ball hits the head pin, which hits the 2; the 2 hits the 4; and the 4 hits the 7.
2. Ball hits the 3; the 3 hits the 6; and the 6 drives into the 10.
3. Ball hits the 5 and the 9; and the 5 hits the 8.

Figure 54 shows an instructor demonstrating the hook ball. Notice the position of the hand at the instant the ball is released. The wrist is rigid, not broken, and the fingers are "closed" to apply the lift straight up for hook spin. As the ball slides off the thumb, the fingers lift counterclockwise to impart the hook spin or lift to the ball.

As you look down on the ball, your thumb position must be between the 10 o'clock and 10:30 positions. This places the fingers between the 4 and 5 o'clock

54. Hand position for the hook

positions (see figure 55). With the thumb hole in the center of the ball, the second joint of the thumb will be pointed towards 10 o'clock.

Figure 56 shows four bowlers who roll very good hooks. Notice the stiff wrist, the finger position at 4:30, the thumb sliding out first followed by the "closed" fingers, and the split-second lift counterclockwise. Keeping the index

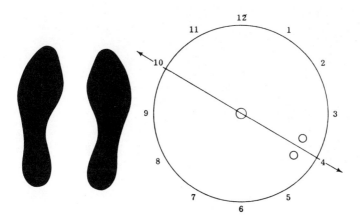

55. Thumb hole at 10 o'clock

56. Good hook rollers

and little finger in close to the middle and ring fingers will help you keep the wrist rigid. Bear down on the ball with the index and little finger.

A "turn-and lift" hook is illustrated in figure 57. Notice how this bowler rotates the wrist counterclockwise while lifting with the fingers at the same time, which motions give this hook its name. This type of hook is harder to control, and it requires much more practice to achieve accuracy. The two rows of white tape on the ball show clearly how the ball track (the surface of the ball making contact with the lane) turns because of the wrist turn.

57. "Turn-and-lift" hook

The majority of better bowlers today roll a turn-and-lift hook like the one shown in figure 57. This is not like the exaggerated power ball thrown by the crankers shown in figure 58. This is just a smooth turn-and-lift semi-roller. There is no better practitioner of this than Earl Anthony.

The big problem for a bowler trying to develop this turn and lift is the probability of *over-turning,* as shown in figure 128, p. 145.

Turn-and-Lift "Cranker"

It's obvious that this is the "era of the cranker." While most bowlers will *not* benefit from trying to crank the ball to gain extra hook spin, we should at least examine the cranking technique.

To crank the ball is to impart more hook spin from *both* the split-second rotation of the wrist as well as from finger lift. There was a time when the "turn-and-lift" cranker could develop too much hooking power to be consistently effective.

Illustrated in figure 58 is a sequence of two power balls thrown by a right-hander and a left-hander. These bowlers throw hard, and the sequence camera has caught the split-second wrist turn and finger lift that imparts an almost unbelievable rotational velocity (revs) as the ball is delivered.

Notice the piece of white tape that was placed under the finger holes. The tape shows the fingers moving from the 6 o'clock position to the 4:30 position for the right-hander and the 6 o'clock to the 7:30 position for the left-hander in a distance less than the bowler's shoe length. The complete turn-and-lift hook spin is applied in about one-thirtieth of a second. Small wonder that few bowlers are physically able to do this. I certainly *do not* recommend this style for the once- or twice-a-week bowler.

The majority of strong crankers are *set* at the line when they apply turn and lift. For example, notice the position of the ball and the distance of the front foot from the foul line in figure 58a.

The set foot is not an absolute requirement, as there are some who can apply the crank as the front foot slides to the foul line. Slide or no slide, the cranker's concentration is on the wrist and fingers, which generate the hook spin. Balance and leverage are the keys to an effective and consistent turn-and-lift hook.

Cranking is not for everyone. Even if the bowler is physically strong enough, it is very difficult to master, and there is always the possibility of over-turning the wrist, resulting in a less effective spinner.

The bowlers in figure 58 roll hundreds of lines per month to maintain consistency and accuracy. The pros have similar practice regimens. The typical league bowler might not bowl enough to reap a benefit from the technique and could actually hurt his or her game in the long run by joining the crankers.

It is the opinion of the authors that permanent physical injury from stress to the body during long-term practice and use of an intense turn-and-lift "cranker" may result, especially among those who develop this style at a very early age such

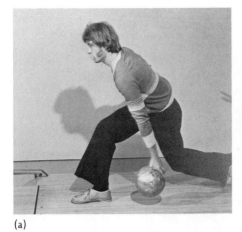
(a)

(d)

(b)

(e)

(c)

(f)

58. Powerful turn-and-lift crankers

59. Young cranker

as the youngsters in figures 59 and 60. Some longtime crankers have experienced such injuries of the back, spine, and the wrist.

The Curve Ball. The curve ball is merely an exaggerated hook. In fact, any slowly rolled good hook will curve in a wide arch. It is not recommended because it presents too many problems of control.

60. Young cranker

Figure 61 shows the left-hander applying the hook lift. The difference is merely that the lift is counterclockwise by the right-hander, clockwise by the left-hander.

The bowlers shown in figure 62 roll very good slight hooks. Notice the fingers are lifting the ball from the 5:30 position. The tape was placed on the ball to determine the precise angle from which the ball was given lift.

61. Left-hander's hook

62. Very good slight hooks

This is the amount of hook we recommend for the bowler who can only handle a lighter ball. It is also recommended for the once-a-week bowler. Less hook, less to control, yet the ball is driving from right to left.

9. PLAYING THE TIGHT LINE

A bowler must possess three extremely important skills to successfully play the inside or tight line. These skills are:

1. A good rolling ball with enough finishing power to combat the added deflection when hitting the pocket from the inside angle.
2. A consistent stroke so the ball will be delivered on the same board at the foul line and the target board on the lane.
3. The ability to approach the foul line from left to right and finish with the slide foot on the same board each time.

Deflection is the change in the path of the ball due to the striking of a bowling pin. Unquestionably, the more the bowler moves his or her line to the left, the more the ball will deflect to the right when hitting the pocket. That's simply physics. Combine with the problem of accuracy, this factor makes the tight line difficult for the average bowler.

When the pros play the tight line, you will generally notice more corner-pin leaves when they don't strike. Several factors combine to produce the corner leave, such as improper timing, inadequate hook spin and roll, or excessive speed. Combined with the difficult angle to the pocket, it is easy to see that the inside line is a very delicate shot.

The pros occasionally leave pocket splits from the tight angle, but that possibility is lessened when a bowler throws a strong finishing ball as in figure 63. The cranker-type hook (turn-and-lift) is especially evident in figures 58, 59, and 60.

The stroke consists of perfect timing, balance, and delivery form as depicted in the illustrations in figure 63. The components of the stroke are the basic tools a bowler must perfect in order to score consistently from deep inside. With these tools, the bowler can consistently play the inside line, as outlined by the tape on the lane. The illustrations show the bowler keeping the ball 1 inch to the right of the tape all the way.

Just as important, the bowler must have the ability and confidence to approach the foul line from left to right and finish with his or her slide foot on the same board every time. Referring again to the tape on the lane (figure 63), the bowler sights for the main target, which is the eighteenth board from the right at the arrow. At the beginning of the approach, his ball would be fifteen boards *from the left* if he held the ball at his side (63a). At the release point at the foul line (63c), the ball hits the lane on the eighteenth board from the left, which should act like the rear sight of a rifle. This rear sight is just as important as his main target

63. Playing the tight line

at the arrows, yet he must hit it by instinct. True, no matter what line you play, you still have an instinctive foul-line target to roll over. However, it's simply more difficult to hit when approaching from left to right, especially since a small variation in the left-to-right approach could cause a corresponding change in the line of the ball.

Next time you run into difficulties playing the tight line, give some thought to the foul-line target. It is just as important as the one you're aiming at beyond the foul line.

III

COMMON FAULTS AND HOW TO CORRECT THEM

10. THE THREE INSTRUCTIONAL METHODS

Three important instructional and corrective tools are available to both the novice and experienced bowler, and the instructor: *the trial swing, the dry run,* and the *one-step delivery.*

The Trial Swing

Two things are vital to your understanding of the *trial swing:* (1) the feet are never moved during the trial swing and (2) the ball is never rolled.

The bowler's feet are stationary while his arm makes a complete *out, down, back,* and *forward* motion (also see figures 7 and 9). This trial swing is basic for beginning instruction and is an invaluable aid in overcoming faults as they develop. Like the approach and delivery, the trial swing is individual. Use whatever stance and ball position is comfortable for you—chest-high, waist-high, or stoop-over stance. Just push the ball out from your regular stance position, swing it down and back, then forward, returning to the starting position, as the bowler in figure 64 is doing. Be sure you understand what is meant by the trial swing, because it is referred to repeatedly throughout this manual.

The Dry Run

The *dry run* is illustrated in figure 65. The dry run (or trial run) is simply the complete approach from the stance position to the delivery *without using the ball.* Like the trial swing, it is invaluable for correcting various faults.

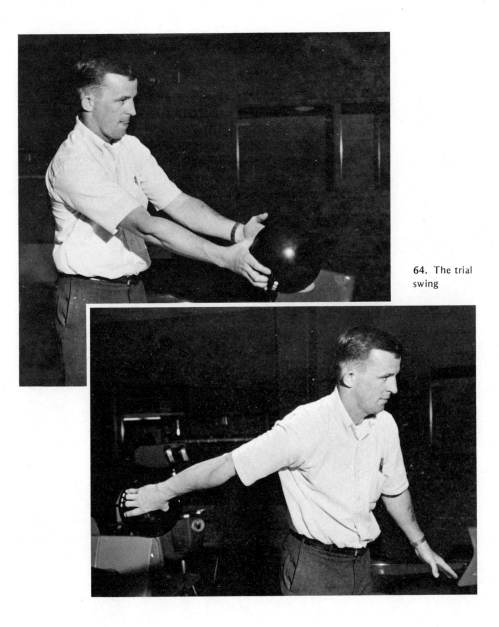

64. The trial swing

The One-Step Delivery

The *one-step delivery* is illustrated in figures 66 and 67. This maneuver is in essence the last step of the approach. Like the trial swing and the dry run, it is used in the correction of many faults. To execute the one-step delivery, carry the ball to within four feet or so of the foul line. Take your normal stance position, putting

65. The dry run

your weight on the foot opposite the sliding foot (a right-hander will have his or her weight on the right foot, a left-hander on the left foot). Swing the ball down and back into the backswing without moving the feet, then come forward with the ball and the slide foot *at the same time,* as shown in figure 67.

66. One-step delivery without the ball

67. The one-step delivery with the ball

Bowlers often have difficulty getting the hang of the one-step delivery. Doing it first without the ball will make it much easier. Also, practicing this method at home using a steam iron or a similar object will help considerably. The one-step delivery is explained in detail in chapter 1 (figure 10).

These methods are appropriate for teaching beginners and for correcting faults of the experienced bowler, because it is easier to take one step and deliver the ball correctly than it is to take four or five. It is much easier to take the trial swing from a stationary position than it is to swing the ball in the pendulum while taking steps. It is easier to learn and develop good timing and delivery form by practicing the approach first without the ball.

11. CORRECTION OF FAULTS: APPROACH

When working on correction of specific faults, make sure that they are corrected in the order of their overall importance. That is to say, approach-timing problems must be remedied first, then delivery form, then hand position, ball roll, and so on. For example, it will be unrewarding to spend time on improving the hook roll when you can't roll the ball the same place twice because of poor delivery form.

Like any other athlete, a bowler can be plagued by numerous problems or faults, some minor, some major. Even a bowler who learned to bowl from a competent instructor and who appears to do everything correctly may suddenly develop a fault.

This chapter covers the most common faults and explains how you can correct them yourself. However, it is preferable that an instructor assist you in the corrections.

If you know what your fault is, check it in the following sections. This section deals with problems in the approach, the next section with the delivery, followed by problems with the roll of the ball.

One word of advice: do not bowl for score when working to correct a fault or to improve your form. Usually your score will suffer during this process, so disregard the score temporarily. In fact, it is preferable to have the pins removed from the machine.

When your approach, delivery, and ball roll are satisfactory, you need only practice to improve your game. Practice will give you the *consistency* that is the secret of better bowling. It is relatively easy to learn to bowl, but to master it, like any other sport, requires much practice, patience, and perseverance.

The technique of bowling is about eighty percent approach timing (the coordination of the foot movements to the arm swing), fifteen percent delivery form (the position of the body at the foul line as the ball is released), and five percent ball roll (the advantages and disadvantages of a particular kind of hook). Thus it is clear that you should consider your approach first, then your delivery position, and finally the ball or hand position.

Approach Timing

If you are a beginner and are having trouble with your timing, bear in mind that the steps, assuming you are right-handed and have adopted a four-step approach, are *right, left, right, left,* in coordination with the pendulum swing of *out, down, back, forward* (*left, right, left, right* for left-handers). If your pendulum swing is free and easy and without hesitation, say the steps aloud to yourself—"right, left, right, left," or "one, two, three, four"—as you approach the foul line. Remember that the steps must coincide with the pendulum swing in order to have a smooth, rhythmic approach.

If your steps appear to be too fast for the arm swing, experiment with another stance. For example, try a lower stance. Often a bowler will delay at the top of the backswing. For a probable remedy, experiment with a *lower* backswing by holding the ball lower in the stance position.

Many times a beginner will suddenly develop the habit of carrying the ball for two steps without knowing why timing has gone sour. Remember that the ball goes *out* on the first step, *down* on the second step, and you will usually eliminate the problem of carrying the ball. In most cases if you can get the first two steps properly coordinated, you can forget close attention to the third and fourth steps. They will nearly always be satisfactory, since the ball will have to go up in the last phase of the backswing arc on the third step, and down and forward on the fourth.

The beginner's timing problem, unlike the experienced bowler's, is not one of finesse. As a beginner with a four-step approach, don't expect more than a rough *out-down-back-forward* coordination. The fluid, graceful approach must be developed through practice. You can speed up your development of a smoother, more fluid pendulum swing by taking trial swings and counting aloud the four beats. Counting aloud will help you regulate the speed of the steps to fit your arm swing.

The timing problem for the advanced student or experienced bowler is another story. The two most common mistakes are taking the steps too quickly and forcing the forward swing. The bowler who charges the foul line can slow down the steps by counting the four beats in the tempo that feels in time with a natural pendulum arm swing. If the forward swing is being forced, the bowler must remember to not "muscle" the ball forward on the last step.

When you are bowling well, count to the rhythm of the arm swing so that you know the tempo of your approach as it should be. Then when you lose that good timing you will spot the error immediately. Since timing is the most important factor in skillful bowling, you will want to know exactly what it should feel like when it is correct. This is somewhat like humming a tune to yourself if you want to dance and there is no music. Count your steps to yourself as you make the approach, and you will learn to recognize the speed-up of a step just as dancers would immediately recognize a change of tempo in music.

Better bowling requires consistency. Consistency of footwork is of vital importance if the tempo of the approach is to be the same each time. The black ball marks on the runway just back of the foul line are the signs of inconsistent footwork, the result of poor timing. The bowler's feet arrived at the foul line before the arm was in position to deliver the ball. The arm swing was accelerated in an attempt to catch up; but it didn't quite make it and the ball was dropped or forced. Whatever you call it, poor timing of the footwork with the arm swing will cause the ball to leave the hand before it can be delivered out onto the lane beyond the foul line.

The most overworked phrases in bowling—"Pitch the ball out"; "You're dropping the ball"; and "You're forcing the ball"—all imply the same thing: the approach is not properly coordinated and the slide foot is consequently arriving at the foul line before the ball. The length of the slide will vary depending on the approach speed, the bowler's height and weight, and so on. Some bowlers have no perceptible slide at all. Their style enables them to maintain balance during the delivery without one. Proper balance during the delivery is the important consideration, not the length of the slide.

Forcing the Forward Swing

This fault is perhaps the most prevalent of all approach and delivery problems. It bothers both the experienced and the beginning bowler. It is the first thing that should be checked if you are having trouble with your game.

Forcing the forward swing may be defined as exerting more arm effort than is needed from the top of the backswing to the point of releasing the ball. The forced forward swing may also be caused by a high backswing. It's not unusual for a backswing that is too high to cause delay at the top, thus forcing the forward swing.

Another reason for a forced forward swing is the attempt to produce something "extra," such as trying to apply more hook spin to the ball, or an overemphasis on pitching the ball out onto the lane, or simply trying for added speed.

Dropping the ball, which causes the black marks on the runway behind the foul line, is caused in almost all cases by forcing or driving the forward swing. This is a vicious cycle in bowling. An experienced bowler will know that the ball is being dropped at the foul line; yet, in an effort to "really pitch the ball out" to correct the mistake, the forward swing will invariably be forced and the ball will continue to be dropped. The ball must be delivered out beyond the foul line *without unnecessary force* so that firm fingers can apply the all-important split-second lift to the ball. Bowlers should constantly keep in mind that the ball is *rolled,* not thrown.

The bowler in figure 68, in trying for "extra lift," forced the forward swing so much that the ball was dropped nearly three feet back of the foul line. Forcing the ball contributed to the stiff knee. The more he tried to pitch the ball out, the more it dropped back of the line.

To correct a forced forward swing, first take the stance position and, without moving the feet, take a trial swing and count "one, two, three, *easy*." The speed of the count must be the same as the speed of the arm swing and the steps in the ap-

68. A four-step bowler: before

proach. After one or two trial swings, take the normal approach and deliver the ball. The counts of "one, two, three" will be synchronized with the first three steps, since no change will be made up to that point. The concern here is the forward swing. Do not force it as the ball goes forward, down, and through. Bring the ball down in the forward swing by its own weight and momentum; do not "muscle" it forward. Figure 69 shows clearly the smooth forward swing, good balance, and pitching the ball out past the foul line that resulted when the bowler "reminded" himself with the simple word "easy."

69. A four-step bowler: after

70. Delivering the ball beyond the foul line

If you are not able to make the correction using the above method, you will have to use the one-step delivery. The one-step delivery is good practice for this problem, because forcing will cause a complete loss of balance. The bowler simply must ease up and *roll the ball* (stroke it) smoothly, in order to remain in balance. By alternating the one-step delivery and the regular approach and delivery, a few practice games should eliminate the tendency to force the ball.

If you are having trouble delivering the ball out onto the lane, a simple measure that often works is to remind yourself to hold onto the ball a split second longer than you have been doing. Using a towel across the foul line for this practice, as shown in figure 70 will also help. This exercise often eliminates the tendency to force the forward swing and consequently to drop the ball. Moving the target closer (try the dots) may eliminate the tendency to force the ball.

Ahead of the Ball

"Ahead of the ball" is the most overworked phrase in bowling, but it describes a very common problem. To be ahead of the ball simply means that the slide foot arrives at the foul line before the ball. Being ahead of the ball and forcing the forward swing are the two biggest headaches for better bowlers. Figure 71 shows a bowler who was ahead of the ball by a half step, and who forced the swing in order to catch up. As a result, he dropped the ball behind the foul line.

To correct this fault, first try counting steps in the tempo that feels proper for the approach. Take a few dry runs to help slow down the steps. If you cannot make this correction on your own, ask your instructor for assistance.

First, the instructor will watch you closely as you take a few dry runs to make certain that you are not rushing to the foul line. Count aloud in the proper tempo. The instructor will count at the same tempo. As soon as you are swinging

71. "Ahead of the ball" by a half step

the ball freely and easily in the proper tempo, the instructor will ask you to do a full approach, again counting to help maintain the proper tempo.

Figure 72 shows the bowler in figure 71 after the correction was made. Notice especially how the ball and the foot arrived at the foul line for the split-second lift and roll at precisely the same moment.

Being ahead of the ball can also be caused by carrying the ball, that is, not allowing the ball to swing freely in the arm swing. Delaying the swing causes the slide foot to arrive at the foul line ahead of the arm swing. A correction for carrying the ball is suggested later in this section.

72. Corrected timing

73. Ahead of the ball

All styles that appear to be ahead of the ball cannot be placed in the same category. A good bowler may have a normal, coordinated approach to the foul line, and be in balance as the ball comes down and through without effort or loss of control, yet appears to be ahead of the ball. This is a separate style not to be confused with the bowler who forces the downswing at the last second. The bowler in figure 73 does not have the coordination to bring the ball forward without forcing it, and he drops the ball. On the other hand, the bowler in figure 74 has complete control of his timing, balance, and leverage, and thus is able to roll a powerful ball.

74. Perfect timing from set position, called "cranking" the ball

Carrying the Ball

The mistake of carrying the ball is sometimes referred to as having a "loafed pendulum swing." This bothers beginners who may carry the ball because they become overcautious when attempting to remember all the points of their game that they are trying to improve. Also many average bowlers make the mistake when they become overcautious in a tight game. Experienced bowlers sometimes "get lazy" on a simple shot and carry the ball as a result of not giving full attention to their swing.

Once the push-away has started, *the ball must be kept in motion* until it is released. The speed of the natural pendulum swing must not be altered by slowing the swing or by carrying the ball during any phase of the swing. Usually the bowler who slows the swing or carries the ball during any part of the natural out-down-

75. Carrying the ball

back-forward rhythm will force the forward swing to attempt to regain timing. Remember: the swing must be smooth like the pendulum of a clock.

Carrying the ball also happens when bowlers make the mistake of concentrating too much on laying the ball out onto the lane rather than swinging it out past the foul line. Too much emphasis on a smooth delivery can be a serious error, since it can cause the loss of much-needed speed on the ball. Always release the ball out on the lane.

The bowler illustrated in figure 75 is completely out of time. Because he was too cautious with his swing, he carried the ball, which causes a forced forward swing. This probably had a bearing on the crooked arm, although there are some bowlers who are strong enough to bend the elbow with no loss of timing, power, or accuracy.

To correct the fault of carrying the ball, stand in the normal stance position and take a few trial swings until the swing is smooth and without hesitation. As you take these trail swings, count the swing rhythm to yourself—"one, two, three, four"—if you have a four-step approach (or, "one, two, three" if you take three steps). Merely add a little zip to your push-away and downswing, and don't loaf or lag. You must have a smooth, rhythmic swing. The trial swing is definitely the cure for this problem. You should count in the same rhythm for your steps, so that they will fit in with the arm swing for perfect timing when you do a regular approach. Now take your regular approach and delivery, and count in the same rhythm as before. This should correct nearly all cases of carrying the ball. If not, you may need the assistance of your instructor as shown in figure 8.

Although the bowler in figure 76 is just a beginner, his timing is now very good. You may notice that he is dropping the right knee too low, and his hand posi-

76. Corrected timing

tion could be improved. Here again, the most prominent fault had to be corrected first. The bowler now has good timing, a higher backswing, and with it, the added natural speed that he formerly lacked.

A Hesitation in the Approach

A hesitation in the approach can be corrected by applying the rule, *fit the steps to the natural arm swing,* not the arm swing to the steps. The hesitation generally occurs after the first or third steps of a four-step approach. This hesitation destroys the natural timing and cuts down on the speed of the ball.

To correct the hesitation, go back to the basic instruction for developing the arm swing and the steps. First, take a trial swing and concentrate on a free-and-easy swing without a hesitation. Next, take a dry run and count the steps to yourself. After three or four dry runs, take your normal approach and deliver the ball. If you are unable to correct the hesitation on your own, have your instructor stand beside you and count to four in the proper tempo to your steps. Repeat the three operations—first, the arm swing without a hesitation, then the steps without hesitation, followed by your normal approach and delivery of the ball. It should not take you long to make this correction with your instructor assisting you.

Sometimes the delay or hesitation in the backswing is difficult to correct because the backswing is too high. In this case, refer to the method for correcting the high backswing described in a later section.

A Hop or Rush in the Approach

If a bowler has a hop or an acceleration of the steps during the next-to-the-last step of the approach, the cause is one step too many. This is not unusual. Illustrated in this section are two bowlers with a "three-step swing and four-step approach," and a bowler who has a "four-step swing and a five-step approach."

The "before" pictures clearly show the hop on the next-to-last step. The bowler in figure 77 chose to change his approach to three steps and keep the same pendulum swing. The bowler in figure 78 preferred the four-step approach, and the bowler in figure 79 also chose the four-step approach.

77. (a) Before

77. (b) After

In figure 77a notice the hop (short step) as this left-handed bowler goes from the second step to the third in the "before" pictures. Now compare that approach with that in the "after" pictures (figure 77b). By eliminating the extra step, his timing, smooth steps, and balance provide a good three-step approach and a balanced body position at the foul line.

Notice the hop, the extremely high backswing, and the poor balance of the bowler in figure 78. Bringing the ball down to the bottom of the arc on the first step is definitely a three-step swing. Because the bowler wanted the four-step approach, it was recommended that her push-away be *straight out*. However, she felt more comfortable with it moving slightly upward (figure 78b). The important key is that she did not lunge or hop on the second step. In figure 78b, she has a relatively smooth approach and good ball speed.

78. (a) Before

78. (b) After (cont.)

The bowler in figure 79a has a four-step swing and a five-step approach. We see this fairly often; especially when bowlers attempt to emulate the pros. This bowler actually hopped approximately 8 inches to the right on his last step! Rather than change the stance and push-away, the correction was a change to four steps, which eliminated the hop and timing flaws (figure 79b).

79. (a) Before

79. (a) Before (cont.)

79. (b) After

79. (b) After (cont.)

79. (c) Straight approach

Crooked Walk to the Foul Line (Drifting)

A bowler should start and finish the approach on or near the same board. There are three problem deviations from the straight line of walk: some bowlers angle from right to left on the way to the foul line, some go from left to right, and others approach in a crooked line. Many champions employ a drift during the approach, but the preferred and most consistent approach is the straight line. Those champions who drift in the approach have learned through constant practice to be consistent. That is certainly the hardest way, and it is not recommended. Early correction of the fault of drifting will profit the bowler in the long run.

Generally, the bowler who aims directly at the pins (a pin bowler) will have a tendency to drift more than the one who aims at the range finders (a spot bowler). It is likely that nine out of ten bowlers who drift on the approach are pin bowlers. Drifting is frequently a problem for the bowler who may attempt to take advantage of the outside line to get a better angle and less deflection on a strike delivery. However, the drift may destroy the line and thus the pocket will be missed.

The crooked approach is so impossible to control that no one uses it intentionally. To correct a crooked approach, note the boards on which you start and finish. (All bowlers should periodically check where they are finishing, particularly after delivering a bad ball.) Your instructor or a qualified observer can point out at which step you drift during the approach. You will not be able to see this. A chalked line, using an erasable chalk, or a taped line can indicate a line on which the feet should be placed during a straight approach (see figure 79c).

Often a crooked approach is not easy to correct and will require much time and patience. If the crooked approach is not the result of another fault (such as rolling a ball that is too heavy, or side-wheeling during the delivery), practice concentrated on eliminating drift is the only solution. You simply will have to slow down and concentrate on *footwork* more than any other phase of the game until a straight walk is developed.

12. CORRECTION OF FAULTS: THE DELIVERY

Failing to Face Straight Ahead

Facing straight ahead means having the shoulders and the hips perpendicular to a line from the bowling shoulder to the point of aim (see figure 80). This means that the shoulders and hips are parallel with the foul line at the moment the ball is released. We say "face straight ahead" as a general direction, but the true meaning is "face straight towards your target with the shoulders and hips perpendicular to the intended line of the ball." The target is approached in a straight line from stance to foul line regardless of the angle being played.

80. Facing straight ahead

81. Shoulders perpendicular to the ball's line

The value of perfect bowling form cannot be overemphasized. It is very important to have the trunk of the body lined up so that the bowling shoulder is directly over the intended path of the ball. Retain this fundamental form regardless of bowling style. Figure 81 illustrates different styles which are excellent.

Keeping the right shoulder over the line or path of the ball is emphasized even more when the bowler finds it necessary to play out and in, or "swing the ball," as the bowler in figure 81 is doing. In this illustration, his line is the fifteen board at the foul line to the twelve board at the arrows. Because of the perfect knee bend, balance, and the straight pendulum swing, he is able to place the ball perfectly over his intended line. It is obvious the bowler illustrated in figure 83 would have difficulty being consistent if he had to play this angle.

The key fundamental is more evident when you study the picture of the bowler in figure 84, who is playing the 10-pin. Playing the left-to-right angle, notice how the body position has the right shoulder directly over the ball's intended line.

82. Excellent examples of facing straight ahead

83. Shoulders and hips not parallel to the foul line

Incidentally, many people emphasize keeping the shoulder up as the ball is released. Actually, nearly all skilled bowlers dip the bowling shoulder slightly as they release the ball. It is not a fault, as seen by checking the bowler in figure 81. It is natural for the weight of the ball to pull the holder down a slight degree. It is a fault and a problem, however, when the bowler *turns* and dips the shoulder. This problem is illustrated by the bowler in figure 83.

Facing straight ahead makes it easier to keep the pendulum swing on a straight line to the target than when the shoulders and hips are turned (figure 83). The bowler cannot turn the shoulders exactly the same amount each time and therefore cannot be consistently accurate. It is similar to shooting a rifle; you cannot shoot accurately if the rear sight moves to the left or right (see figure 85). In bowling, the shoulder joint acts as the pivot point for the pendulum. Keeping the pivot point directly over the path intended for the ball will improve accuracy. The bowler who twists and turns at the foul line will invariably pull the ball. This causes the pendulum to swing and the ball to be released at an angle instead of directly over its intended path or line.

To correct the tendency to turn sideward as the ball is delivered, bend the knee and put the weight of the body on the forward foot. When emphasis is placed only on bending the front knee, some bowlers will rear back as they deliver the ball and lose their balance, which at best substitutes one fault for another. Keep the toe

84. Playing the 10-pin

85. Inconsistent line of flight

of the shoe on the floor to act as a rudder and to prevent the back leg from swinging around to the side. A full rubber sole on the right shoe is an invaluable "brake" to stop the back leg from swinging to the side. A rubber tip on the toe of the shoe

86. (a) Toes straight ahead   (b) Left foot pointed straight ahead

may be used for the same purpose. The bowler shown in figure 86 is the same bowler in figure 83 after the correction was made.

To correct the fault of not facing straight ahead, first take a dry run. If you cannot square the shoulders and hips without the ball, you cannot do so with the ball. Take as many trial runs as you need until you feel that you can deliver the ball with the body in balance and the shoulders and hips parallel to the foul line.

The one-step delivery, explained in detail in section 10, is the best cure for correction of poor delivery form. To work on a problem that requires the dry run and the one-step delivery, bowl on a lane away from other bowlers. Have the pins removed from the pin deck, if possible. First, take a one-step delivery. While you wait for the ball to return, take a dry run. Then take your complete approach and deliver the ball. Repeat this sequence until the shoulders and hips are parallel to the foul line at the moment of releasing the ball.

You can check yourself by looking straight down over your front knee after releasing the ball. If your toes point straight ahead, and your body is still and posed, you are in balance and facing straight ahead. Notice how many of the top bowlers pose momentarily after releasing the ball, as shown in figure 87. It is very easy for this bowler to check his balance and be sure that he is facing straight ahead.

Loss of Balance During the Delivery

Balance during the delivery depends on the left knee bend (the right knee for left-handers), toes pointed straight ahead, and the weight of the body shifted almost entirely to the front foot. Proper balance and facing straight ahead are closely related. In general, a bowler who faces straight ahead will maintain balance throughout the delivery. Therefore, the method used to correct flaws in balance is the same as that used for failure to face straight ahead.

87. Pose after releasing the ball

Good balance as the ball is delivered is important in several ways. Aside from the obvious problems that loss of balance can cause, it contributes to other faults, such as side-wheeling, turning to the right (to the left for left-handers), and many others. You will find bowlers who complain that their foot sticks as they attempt to slide to the foul line. This trouble can be traced to loss of balance. The heel on the slide foot has made firm contact with the approach instead of allowing the slide to continue on the sole of the shoe.

Bear in mind that you build up considerable momentum during the approach. An unbalanced delivery makes it very difficult to stop smoothly behind the foul

88. Before: loss of balance and turning during delivery

line. Bend the front knee, and the upper part of the body will move forward and come to a balanced stop automatically. This delivery form also will eliminate lofting the ball, since the ball will be released only a few inches above the floor and beyond the foul line.

The bowler shown in figures 88, 89, and 90 is a good example of *turning* and *poor leverage at the line*. Figure 89 shows the correction that was made using the *dry run* and the *one-step delivery*. Figure 90 shows the same bowler after correction. All that is required is a little practice and patience.

89. Instructor encouraging the follow-through

90. After: balance maintained throughout delivery

The bowler illustrated in figures 88-90 is a very good example of "before" and "after" delivery form. It doesn't require much work to develop the proper form, just a little patience and understanding of the value of sound delivery fundamentals. In this case, the one-step delivery corrected the fault. Figure 89 shows the instructor working with the bowler. This help was necessary to encourage the follow-through and facing straight ahead with the body posed and in balance. The "after" picture, figure 90, speaks for itself.

Lofting the Ball

Lofting the ball is what we call throwing the ball several feet beyond the foul line from a nearly standing position. Aside from being very hard on the lanes, from the bowler's viewpoint it is objectionable because it does not produce good ball roll and action.

Lofting generally is caused by the bowler not bending the front knee in the delivery, the ball being too light, or the thumb hole being too tight. A different ball will correct the latter causes of lofting. To correct not bending the front knee, the simple one-step delivery is the cure.

In figure 91 the bowler did not bend the forward knee. This upright and stiff position caused the ball to loft and caused the bowler to "fall" off balance at the foul line. Repeated practices through use of the one-step delivery resulted in new habits of bending the forward knee and a solid position at the foul line as the ball was released (figure 92).

91. Before

92. After

Dropping the Shoulder

Many bowlers struggle to "keep the shoulder up." Pictures of the best, such as the bowler in figure 93, would show that the ball pulls the shoulder slightly downward. A slight drop of the shoulder is not a problem *as long as the bowling shoulder is on a line with your target.* Bend the forward knee and keep the front foot pointed toward the path or line to the target. Only the very powerful and strong can keep the shoulder from dropping slightly.

93. A slight drop of the shoulder

Crooked Pendulum Swing

The crooked pendulum swing is *swinging the ball outside a straight line* to the desired target, whether board (spot), line, or pin aiming, during the out-down-back-forward pattern of the pendulum arm swing.

A crooked pendulum arm swing that results in poor and inaccurate ball delivery can be caused from a faulty push-away and downswing, or during the back-swing by bringing the ball behind the body, or from swinging the ball outward, away from the body. If the fault is in the push-away and downswing it is relatively easy to correct. In the stance, hold the ball slightly to the right of your waistline as you face the pins. Left-handed bowlers will hold the ball in this relative position on the left side of the body. Keep the elbow near the side of the body. Do repeated trial swings starting from the stance position. Check the position before each practice swing. Check and observe the hand and ball position throughout the push-away and as the arm moves through the downswing. Do not allow the wrist to turn at any time during the delivery, keep it firm and "locked." Keep the ball moving on a straight line that coincides with the intended pathway to the target throughout the entire pendulum arm swing.

After the stance and the trial swing are smooth, alternate practice of a trial swing followed by a one-step delivery. Recall that this simulates the last step of the approach and the delivery of the ball. When the push-away and pendulum swing technique is rhythmic and has become habit, practice it in the full approach and delivery of the ball.

The bowler in figure 94 illustrates the crooked pendulum swing. In figure 95 the pendulum swing has been improved using the correction methods just described.

94. Before

95. After

Arm Twisting

Some bowlers do not have the necessary strength to keep the arm straight. Many experienced bowlers (crankers) deliberately turn the arm in the backswing and forward swing. It has become part of their style and they are able to do it consistently under all conditions. Nevertheless, the beginnner who twists the arm during the delivery should correct the fault immediately.

To make this correction, be certain that the ball fits perfectly and is the correct weight. Then, in the stance position, take several trial swings, checking that both hands are under the ball for support during the stance. Check the bowling hand closely as the ball starts down from the push-away. If arm twisting during the trial swing can be avoided, the bowler should be able to do the approach, delivery, and release of the ball without any arm twist. If not, the instructor should give assistance as shown in figures 96 and 97.

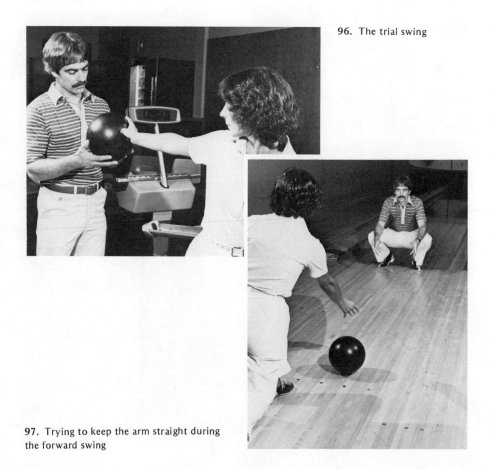

96. The trial swing

97. Trying to keep the arm straight during the forward swing

Use the trial swing and watch the hand position carefully to correct arm twisting in the push-away, the downswing, and the backswing. Figure 95 shows a bowler who twists the arm in the backswing. The instructor catches the ball at the top of the backswing so that the bowler can turn around and observe the mistake. Notice that the arm twist creates the additional fault of turning the shoulders away from being perpendicular to the intended path of the ball.

If the arm is twisted during the foward swing, a different method of correction is necessary. Stand at the head of the approach (see figure 97) with the instructor standing at the foul line. Roll the ball down the approach, concentrating on keeping the arm straight and firm, with no twist. Follow through completely so that you are able to sight over your index finger as you point to the target. Repeat this procedure until the fault is fully corrected. When you are able to bring the ball out, down, back, and forward with your arm firm and straight, take your normal approach and deliver the ball.

If further assistance is needed, the instructor should hold the bowler's wrist and go through the entire approach and delivery as illustrated in figure 98.

98. Instructor assisting in complete approach and delivery

The High Backswing

The high backswing is not in itself a fault. Although a high backswing is not recommended for those bowlers who already have too much power and ball speed, there is nothing wrong with it provided the bowler has good approach timing and delivery form and proper ball speed. Many high-average bowlers, including champions, use a high backswing.

A higher backswing is recommended for those bowlers who need more power, because it gives added speed without unnecessary force or strain. Some bowlers can use additional speed, but it should not be added at the expense of timing or delivery form. If the high backswing causes the hips or shoulders to turn, the bowler should change to a lower backswing. The pivoting may cause dipping and turning, and side-wheeling, two faults that would not be worth the speed gained.

A delay at the top of the backswing can be caused by a backswing that is too high, and this is also not worth the additional speed to be gained.

The bowler illustrated in figures 99a and b displays good timing and delivery form in spite of the high backswing. Figure 99c shows the recommended backswing. Figure 100 shows a bowler who has a high backswing, but he also has too much speed and a small timing problem. He will have to lower the backswing.

99. (a) and (b) High backswing with proper speed and timing

(c) The recommended backswing

100. High backswing with excessive speed and poor timing

To make this correction, first consider timing; holding the ball in a lower stance position may be necessary, or the number or size of steps may have to be changed. These should be tried first. If that does not correct the height of the backswing, ask the instructor for assistance. First take a trial swing from about 4 feet behind the foul line (as in figure 101). As the trial swing is taken, the instructor will stop the ball at the correct height. It may be helpful for the instructor to count aloud the rhythm of your approach.

101. Correcting the high backswing

102. After correcting a high backswing

From this same position on the runway, take a one-step delivery, again counting the cadence of the arm swing. Concentrate on the proper height of the backswing, then on bringing the ball forward, down, and through on the last count. You should have the feel of where the ball is at all times during the count, especially on the last two counts.

Do not hurry this exercise. When you are able to take the one-step delivery without assistance so that it feels easy and smooth, try a dry run or two. Then make your full approach while the instructor watches and makes corrections should you revert to your old style. Figure 102 shows the bowler in figure 100 after he has corrected his high backswing. His backswing is lower, he is relaxed, his forward knee is bent, and his timing is better. The same technique will correct a hesitance in the backswing.

A Hop in the Delivery

Figures 103a and b clearly show the fault of a hop in the delivery. This hop during ball delivery is not uncommon. Although some bowlers with respectable averages have the hop, it is certainly not the easy way to bowl. This bowler delivers the ball well behind the foul line. The timing is off a little, and obviously he must hop to keep from falling.

Correction of this fault is not difficult. Alternate the dry run and the one-step delivery, preferably without using the pins, and *concentrate on bending the knee.* Figure 103c shows the same bowler after he eliminated the hop from his delivery. Note the bend in the knee that provides a solid and balanced position at the foul line.

103. (a) and (b) Before correcting the hop for balance and leverage

(a)

(b)

(c) After correction

A Wide Pendulum Swing (Side-Wheeling)

The inconsistency and inaccuracy that occur because of a wide pendulum swing (side-wheeling) are illustrated in the "before and after" pictures of the bowler shown in figure 104.

This style is not unusual, especially with young bowlers. Young bowlers often learn to bowl with a ball that is heavier than it should be, and may try to put "extra stuff" on the ball. The ball pulls the bowler off course due to his or her lack of strength. It may become a habitual style as the bowler grows older.

This flaw in delivery form is associated with facing straight ahead, which was discussed at the beginning of this chapter. Compare figure 45, page 56, in which the bowler is turned at the line, with figure 105 in which the bowler is parallel with the line. It is obvious that the bowler who can deliver the ball with the arm directly

104. (a) Before

(b) and (c) After

over and on a line with the target will hit the target more consistently. To correct the error, use the same methods described for learning to face straight ahead. Alternate practice of the dry run with the one-step delivery before incorporating a full approach.

It may help considerably in the correction of this fault to move temporarily to the extreme outside of the approach and use the first arrow as the target. Crowding the channel will force you to keep your arm closer to your side. The bowler

105. After

106. Correcting the wide pendulum swing

(a) Wide pendulum swing

(b) and (c) Corrected swing

shown in figure 106a, is a very good example of a wide pendulum swing. Figures 106b and c show the same bowler playing the *outside angle* to make the correction. If possible, work on correcting faults without pins, since any distraction such as concern for pinfall may cause a bowler to revert to old habits.

(a) Dumping the ball

107. Poor follow-through
and correction.

(b) "Reaching for the ceiling"

A Poor Follow-Through

The follow-through and its value were explained in chapter 2. Good timing and delivery form generally ensure a good follow-through, although there are exceptions. Figure 107 shows a bowler whose timing and delivery form are satisfactory, yet she cut off the follow-through by dumping the ball, thereby impairing accuracy, ball roll, and the added natural speed generated by the follow-through.

To correct a poor follow-through, use the one-step delivery and "reach for the ceiling"; let the bowling arm continue all the way up to the side of the head. After a few practice rolls you should be able to follow through correctly.

Ask the instructor to stand on the ball return as illustrated in figure 107b, then reach toward his or her outstretched hand. A few attempts at "shaking hands" in this manner will remind you to swing the arm upward in a full follow-through.

Ball Speed

Bowlers should roll a ball from the foul line to the pins in 2-1/8 to 2-3/4 seconds if they are to get maximum benefit of pin action. The average bowler rolls the ball from the foul line to the pins in 2-1/4 seconds. The exceptions are the powerful crankers described in figure 58. The ball that is delivered too slowly has several disadvantages. In most cases, the energy or power generated by ball spin will have dissipated by the time the ball reaches the pins.

To increase ball speed, experiment with holding the ball higher in the stance. The higher the ball is held, the longer the pendulum and the higher the backswing. When the ball is pushed out and slightly upward during the push-away, the increased length of the arc in the pendulum arm swing will add natural speed.

Some bowlers, however, will lose their timing with this type of push-away. Additional speed can be applied by accelerating the push-away and downswing. This tends to speed up both the arm swing and the steps automatically. Do not try these techniques without your instructor's assistance to prevent loss of correct timing. Accelerating the push-away can easily cause development of a "three-step swing with a four-step approach." The instructor's count and close observation of the coordination of arm and feet will determine the cadence of the steps.

Do not try for added speed by forcing the forward swing or a higher backswing. The higher backswing must result naturally from either of the two methods described above.

The natural speed you want can only be gained by use of the techniques described above, improvement in coordination, which takes practice and patience to develop, or by increased physical strength.

Some bowlers roll a ball from the foul line to the pocket in 4 seconds or more. If 4 seconds is the best a pupil can do—fine! It will do as a beginning.

The "too fast" ball can be difficult to correct, assuming the bowler has natural speed and is not forcing. To slow down the fast ball, the bowler should concentrate on *rolling* the ball instead of throwing it. This will often slow everything down, yet maintain or improve timing and coordination. If this does not work, reduce the height of the backswing, or lower the ball in the stance position. Bear in mind that the shorter the length of the arc, the slower the ball will be delivered, if it is not forced. Concentrate on the speed of the approach. To slow down the approach speed, count your steps in a slower cadence, "one, two, three, four." Make this change carefully because slowing the steps can result in loss of timing. While it is advantageous to reduce the speed of the extremely fast ball, it must be done without impairment of natural timing and coordination. Otherwise one fault may have been corrected at the expense of introducing several others more burdensome than the "too-fast" delivery.

Ball Roll

To determine the position of the fingers the *instant* the ball is released, place a 4-inch piece of tape under the finger holes as shown in figure 108. A fast-ball bowler will have to slow down in order to make the observation. This test clearly

108. Correcting ball roll

shows that the bowler in figure 108a rolls a good straight ball. Notice the tape is exactly at the 6 o'clock position, therefore the ball will roll like a wheel down the lane. On the other hand, the bowler in figure 108b gave the fingers a slight left-to-right lift, causing the fingers to lift from left of the 6 o'clock position. It doesn't take much to make the ball fade to the right (back-up). The bowler in figure 108c and d released the ball with the fingers at the 3 o'clock position. Normally this is a good full roller (see figure 125, p. 143). However, in turning the wrist counterclockwise, while trying to turn and lift or crank, he turned too late, as figure 108c and d shows. This over-turning resulted in a ball that "finishes" weak and ineffective.

Killing the Hook

Not getting the correct hook as the ball is released is called "killing the hook." This can be caused by several things. Generally, the hand is not in the proper position as the ball is released, as described in chapter 2. To roll an effective hook, the fingers *must* be between the 3 and 5:30 o'clock positions as the ball is released, preferably at 4 to 4:30 o'clock. Any other hand position will result in either a straight ball, a near-straight ball, a back-up, a reverse hook, or a spinner.

Even when the fingers are in the proper position, "dumping" the ball on the lane will kill the hook. Dumping the ball is a term for releasing the ball with the fingers and thumb at the same time (see figures 109a and b). The ball slides off

109. (a) and (b) Poor hand position: dumping the ball

(c) and (d) Correction for dumping the ball

the sides of the fingers and the thumb, rather than being released from the pads of the firm fingers. Thus an effective spin as the fingers move upward into the follow-through is lost; the ball's spin and roll is "killed."

Imagine that you are holding a suitcase by its handle and that you want to slide it down the lane to the pins without the suitcase falling over on its side. In order to accomplish this unlikely objective, you would have to release the handle with the fingers and thumb at the same time. If you dump the ball in this way, a pronounced follow-through, with the bowling fingers positioned at 4 to 4:30 as the ball is released, will remind you to lift and not dump the ball (see figures 109c and d.) Be sure that you release the ball out over the foul line and keep the arm on line with the ball's intended pathway.

To roll an effective hook, the thumb must leave the ball first; then the fingers apply the hook spin. Like the pro golfer who can feel the club head hit the ball, the bowler must develop the feel of the fingers lifting the ball the split second it is released. The good bowler concentrates on the position of the fingers and the lift, not on the position of the thumb or thumb hole, because it is easier to visualize the fingers lifting than the correct position of the thumb. The thumb merely guides the ball. Don't squeeze the thumb! This could cause an over-turn.

Figure 110 shows a bowler who has not maintained the correct hand position throughout the delivery. He has applied finger lift to the ball, but he has turned the wrist clockwise so that the lift was from the inside at about 7 o'clock instead of from the outside at about 4 to 5 o'clock. He has rolled a back-up despite the lift by the fingers. The fingers must be on the outside to roll the hook ball.

To correct these faults you must learn to roll the conventional (stiff wrist) hook, not the "turn-and-lift" type. Any maneuver other than a stiff wrist will make

110. Turning the wrist

111. The stiff-wrist hook

correction difficult. Therefore lock your wrist in a stiff position with the middle and ring fingers at 4 to 4:30 o'clock, as illustrated in figure 111. Next, bring the ball up to your starting position, keeping the grip firm so that the wrist will remain rigid and straight. Take several trial swings, observing the wrist and hand closely to make certain the wrist is rigid and the hand is in the proper position. Take the one-step delivery. Repeat this procedure until the hand position is completely satisfactory, and you can feel the ball coming off the two fingers as you lift straight up; maintain fingers at 4:00 to 4:30.

If you are unable to release the ball correctly and you revert to your old fault, call on your instructor for assistance as you take a one step delivery (see figure 112d). You will soon get the feel and develop proper wrist position if the instructor holds your wrist in this manner.

Marking the ball with tape, as illustrated in figure 111, will assist in checking the amount of "turn and finish" on the ball, as well as the position of the ball track, which is the surface on which the ball rolls. A 3-inch piece of white tape directly under the finger holes will show the amount of turn or spin on the ball. The tape on a properly released hook ball will clearly show an acceleration of spin the last 10 to 20 feet before the ball hits the pins. This is referred to as a good *finishing* ball. It will have a minimum of deflection upon contact with the pins.

Study the excellent picture in figure 111 of the fingers coming out of the ball. This type of release and hand position will get you the desired twelve or thirteen complete revolutions from the foul line to the pocket, and will provide maximum mixing action and pinfall.

Too Much Hook or Curve

A combination of a light ball and insufficient speed will cause too much hook or curve.

For the bowler who rolls a light ball slowly down the lane, this can be a big problem. Assuming that everything possible has been done to increase natural speed, and that a 10-pound ball is the heaviest the bowler can handle, he or she will have to be content with these conditions for the present. The amount of curve can be reduced by positioning the hand and wrist so that the thumb points to the 11:30 o'clock position, fingers at the 5:30 position (see figure 62, p. 70) just enough to give the ball a slight lift with the fingers without any wrist turn. It is usually best for bowlers to roll a hook, and it is to be regretted if one loses a natural hook. However, there is no alternative if the hook simply curves beyond control, no matter from what angle it is rolled from the foul line.

To change the hand position so that the thumb is at the 11:30 o'clock position, stand at the head of the approach and repeatedly roll the ball to your instructor standing at the foul line (see figure 113d). When you are able to keep the wrist straight and rigid, roll a ball down the lane. Repeat the entire procedure until you are able to deliver the ball consistently, thereby cutting down the amount of the curve. Watch out for overcorrection. That produces the back-up, which is always a possibility when the thumb position approaches the 11:30 or 12 o'clock position.

Correcting a Poor Hook

A poor hook occurs frequently when a bowler "is positive" that the fingers are lifting the ball from the correct position. Lifting, true, but not from the correct position. Notice at the top of the backswing in figure 112a that the fingers are at approximately the 5 o'clock position. In 112b however, the fingers are now at the 6 o'clock position. The lift and roll were present, but the lift was "too far *behind* the ball." The more that the bowler forces the ball in trying to get the ball to hook, the more the roll of the ball is "killed."

The problem is corrected by using the *trial swing and the one-step delivery.* In figure 112c the bowler does the trial swing while standing in the one-step delivery position. The hook hand position is exaggerated by use of the "suitcase grip" in which the thumb is at 9 o'clock and fingers at 3 o'clock, so that the fingers are on the *side of the ball.* The lack of a straight wrist will be corrected later.

Next, as shown in figure 112d, the instructor holds the wrist of the bowler during the practice of the one-step delivery. After a dozen practice rolls or more, the bowler is able to properly release the ball without further assistance, as shown in figure 112e. After practice-rolling the ball (preferably with pins removed from the deck) alternately using the one-step delivery and the full approach, and still concentrating on the suitcase grip, the bowler gradually firms the wrist. The final result is shown in figure 112F. Remember—*keep the wrist rigid, "squeeze" the fingers, not the thumb.* The thumb just guides the ball.

Generally, it does not require use of all three instruction methods to correct the hand position. It is necessary only when the problem is so habitual that the bowler must return to the basics in order to change.

112. Correcting a poor hook

(a)

(b)

(c)

(d)

(e)   (f)

Correcting the Back-Up

The back-up delivery is ineffective and must be avoided. Usually it results from an improperly delivered straight ball. Also, it is more prevalent among beginners who learn to bowl by rolling the ball down the middle of the lane, as in figure 113a or from the wrong side of the lane. As the back-up is delivered, the thumb, instead of staying at the 12 o'clock position goes over toward the 1 o'clock position (see figure 113b) for right-handed bowlers. This causes the fingers to apply a slight left-to-right rotation to the ball, and it fades to the right as it rolls down the lane. For left-handed bowlers, the thumb goes towards 11 o'clock, which causes the ball to fade toward the left as it rolls. The piece of tape (in a vertical position under the finger holes) does not show in figure 113a because the hand has already turned clockwise; however, figure 113b shows the clockwise movement as the ball rotates.

To be effective, a ball must drive into the pins after contact with the head or target pins. The back-up does just the opposite. It deflects off the head pin much more than the straight ball or the hook ball, and it does not drive in to knock down the 5 pin on a strike ball roll. You cannot roll the back-up ball unless you twist your arm and wrist clockwise (right-handed) as you release the ball. Keeping the arm stiff and straight and the thumb pointed at the 10:30 position will eliminate the back-up. Thus a line drawn between the middle and ring finger would be at the 4:30 or 5 o'clock position. For the left-handed bowler, apply the same relative positions, thumb at 1:30 and fingers at 7:00 to 7:30.

Now hold the ball at your side as shown in figure 113c. Swing the arm back and forth so that you get the "feel" of the hand and wrist in the "shake hands" position. Next, raise the ball to your normal stance position and take a few *trial swings. Do not let the wrist or arm twist or turn.* In most cases, this corrects the back-up. If it doesn't, continue with your instructor as shown in figure 113d. From here move to the one-step delivery, as shown in figure 113e. Repeat the process until you can do it perfectly, as this bowler did in figures 113f and g. If you need further assistance, ask the instructor to hold your wrist firmly in the proper position as you practice the one-step delivery.

113. Correcting the back-up

(a)

(b)

(c)

(d)

(e)

(f)

(g)

130

Over-turning the Wrist

Far too many bowlers make the mistake of trying to *turn and lift* for added hook without instruction. Most end up rolling a dead ball as shown in figure 114.

Look at the "before" picture, figures 114a, 114b, and 114c. Figure 114a shows the tape line under the fingers. Figure 114b shows the tape on top of the ball, with the thumb pointing to 6 o'clock. Figure 114c shows the ball is back-spinning. Backspin on the ball creates the ineffective "dead ball." A return to the basics through the *trial swing* and the *one-step delivery* will help a bowler develop a good rolling "5:30 hook" roll (figures 114d-f).

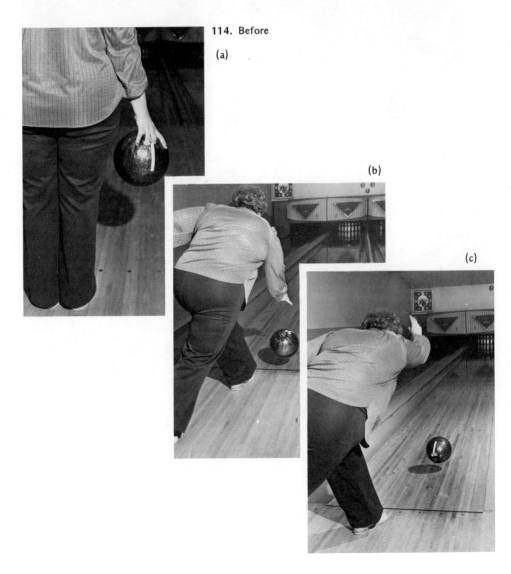

114. Before

(a)

(b)

(c)

114. After

(d)

(e)

(f)

IV

TECHNICAL INFORMATION

13. TAPS AND SPLITS

Taps

When a bowler appears to do everything right—good approach timing, good delivery, good hook rolled solidly into the strike pocket—and still leaves a pin, that is a *tap*. As long as the game of bowling survives, you will hear bowlers lament the taps that robbed them of the big score.

In the following picture sequences, you will notice the painted white lines that border the general pocket area, that is, boards 16, 17, and 18 from the right channel. The illustrated lines allow you to follow the deflection of the ball or lack of it. Left-handed bowlers, look at these illustrations in a mirror to get the perspective for "your side of the lane" and your strike pocket. You will need to mentally reverse the pin numbers (e.g., 10-pin is equivalent to 7-pin).

The ball travels approximately 10-1/2 inches from contact with the head pin until it hits the 3-pin. A slight deflection in this critical area makes a 10-pin tap possible, regardless of the angle at which the ball entered the pocket. Surprisingly, the angle played by the bowler makes very little difference in the pin-fall pattern.

Figure 115 illustrates the 10-pin tap. This is the most common tap for right-handed bowlers. Figure 115a clearly shows the ball hitting the pocket dead center (on the 17 board). Figure 115b shows the ball deflecting approximately one-half inch after it made contact with the head pin. The mere one-half inch of deflection is enough to cause the 10-pin tap. A solid hit like this will produce a strike most of the time. Unfortunately, the bowler did something slightly different on this roll and the ball deflected.

115. The 10-pin tap

116. Solid pocket hit for a strike

Illustrated in figure 116 is another solid pocket hit, but this one carried for a strike. This hit also was on the 17 board, the center of the pocket. In comparing the two hits, the only apparent difference is the one-half inch of deflection on the 10-pin leave, whereas the strike shows the ball hitting the head pin and then driving straight back without deflecting.

Illustrated in figure 117 is a solid 4-pin tap. This particular roll was on the 18 board when it made contact with the head pin. Although "high" hits like this are hardly detected with the naked eye, it is obvious that the ball hit high when you analyze the pin-fall pattern. The pattern differs considerably from the 10-pin leave, and the ball came in just one board higher. All high hits like this 4-pin leave show the head pin must take out the 9-pin, with the 2-pin coming off the kickback to get the 4- and 7-pins. It is simply a matter of luck it seems; sometimes they fall, but sometimes they narrowly miss being hit, as they did in this sequence.

The solid 8-pin tap leaves no room for argument. All experts agree that the solid 8-pin leave is a tap. As illustrated in figure 118, the hit was solid, and the ball was digging hard and fast into the pocket. This tap is caused by the 5-pin chopping *(cherrying off)* the 8-pin. This cherry comes about because an "assist" from the head pin gives the 5-pin a glancing blow, sending it to the right causing it to miss the 8-pin. On most strikes, the head pin hits the 2-pin a glancing blow, then goes straight back with the ball, hitting the 5-pin, the 8-pin, or both. If there is such a thing as a *perfect spot* to hit for a strike, it is the *crack between the 17-18 boards*, as is the case in this solid 8-pin tap (figure 118). With a hit such as this, it is almost impossible to leave a 10-pin.

117. The 4-pin tap

118. The 8-pin tap

You doubtless will hear the statement made that "it was the wrong angle to carry the 10-pin" (or the 4-pin). We don't believe that one angle is much better than another. Where is the angle that will not leave a tap? At best, changing the angle may possibly increase the chance of carrying one particular pin, but it will also decrease the chance of carrying another. All that will have been accomplished is a substitution of one pin for another. However, bowlers can play a good tight line and leave just as many corner pins on good hits as bowlers who play down the fifth board and into the pocket. If a bowler has more confidence from one particular angle than from another, that is the place from which he or she should roll. Bluntly, put your faith in hitting the pocket solidly rather than in the place the ball is rolled from. For the beginner and the average bowler, the second arrow is the recommended target for rolling the strike ball, but if you have more confidence in moving a few boards either way, by all means do so. However, you must bear in mind the condition of the lanes will dictate the best angle to play.

119. Light pocket hit

Pocket Splits and Deflection

All bowlers—champion, average, or beginner—will leave pocket splits. They will also hit the 1-3 pocket and leave the 5-pin, or the 5-8 pins due to the deflection of the ball on contact with pins. Bowlers with better timing and better hook spin and roll on the ball will not leave a pocket split as often as the bowler with poorer timing and poorer ball roll. We could also add that incorrect angle "encourages" the pocket split, such as a straight ball rolled down the center of the lane instead of off the right-hand corner, or a hook played from too far inside when the bowler does not roll a hook strong enough to combat the deflection encountered when the ball contacts the pins. This is especially true if the lanes are a little "fast" (slick from lane oil) and the pins are heavy. Figure 119 shows what appeared to be a good pocket hit, but the ball "quit" (deflected to the right). On a normal strike pattern, the ball hits enough of the 5-pin to drive it into the 8-pin. Any time a bowler, strong hook or average hook, hits the pocket and leaves the 5-7, 5-10, or single 5-pin, it is simply a case of the ball quitting when it hit the 1-3.

The pocket hit shown in figure 119 was a little "light," as can be seen by the ball's position on the 16 board and the tape lines. However, if it had been a good roll the ball would not have deflected the 2 inches or more that this one did. The ball must be to the right of the 14 board in order to miss the 5-pin.

What about the professionals who roll the power or "cranker" ball as described in chapter 2? We would have to say that while the average bowler must "keep the fingers crossed" when the hit is light (15 or 16 board), the power bowlers find it their best chance of striking. Watch them on television! The power ball appears to "blow the pins into the next county" on these light hits.

The 8-10 split in figure 120 was left by a hit dead center in the pocket (17 board). On this particular roll, the bowler simply rolled a bad ball that did not finish strongly enough to resist over-deflection.

120. Pocket split

Other Splits and What to Do About Them

The pocket split is usually caused by a poorly rolled ball, whereas the other splits come from errors of accuracy—usually high on the head pin, or "right on the nose." All splits are provoking, but they are part of the game. Even the best hitters in baseball will hit into a double play now and then.

Unless the game depends on the conversion of the split, we suggest playing it safe by always hitting one pin (or two pins in the case of splits like the 6-7-10). Many a game is lost by one or two pins. If you have a strike preceding the split, *always* get at least half of the split with the second roll. If you should attempt the conversion of the 4-6-7-10, and the ball goes too wide and drops into the channel, you will lose four pins in count. You should, of course, always attempt to make the "little" splits like the 3-10, 4-5, because any reasonable attempt will get at least one pin.

If you or your team is down by a considerable margin in a match or game, then go for broke and try to convert your splits, much as a baseball team trailing by a big margin will go for the big inning, rather than sacrifice to get one run.

One last suggestion: never try to convert the railroads (4-6, 7-10, 8-10, 7-9) by sliding one pin into the other. Because the pins are parallel with absolutely no angle between pins, the chance for this type of conversion is very remote, thus you will miss both pins and lose count for your score. The percentage is better if you try to hit one pin a solid blow, slamming it into the ball cushion in the rear of the pit and hope that it will carom off and into the other pin.

Which Angle Is Best to Play?

In the series of pin-action shots in this chapter, we have attempted to prove that we must accept the fact that the pocket is small (see figure 121) and that bowling is a high-skill sport. The bowling ball is rolled 60 feet down a lane in an attempt to hit an area less than 2 inches wide. When the bowler hits the pocket but the ball was not rolled very well, he or she is subjected to taps and splits. It is truly a game of fractions. A quarter-inch or less can be the difference between glory and frustration. A bowler can, however, play the percentages.

The pin action shown in figures 115 through 120 proves that deflection causes the 10-pin tap, and excessive deflection causes pocket splits and the 5-pin leave. Obviously, then, the outside angle as illustrated in figure 122 will produce less deflection than the inside or tight-line angle. Therefore, the inside angle, or tight line, is only for the bowler who rolls a strong ball.

The bowler in figure 123 is playing the extreme *outside* line or angle. This angle is good for the slight hook and the straight ball; it is especially good for the bowler who does not have much power or strength.

The beginner who plays this angle should avoid the tendency to drift to the left. If the bowler shown here were to drift a board or two to the left, he might hit his target, but the ball would not "come up" to the pocket. Specifically, the bowler

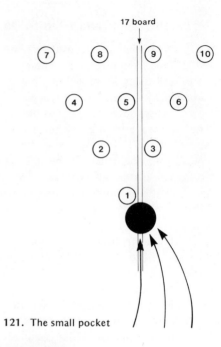

121. The small pocket

122. Tight, normal, and outside angles

123. Playing the outside angle

in figure 123 places the ball on the third board at the foul line, and his target is the first range finder or arrow (the fifth board). But if he placed the ball on the fifth board at the foul line and hit the *same* target, the ball would not "come up" to the strike pocket.

When you have determined the angle of your ball's path, have your instructor or a teammate check whether or not you are placing the ball on the proper foul-line board. You have to rely on their observation since you cannot see this—you are looking at your target out on the lane.

14. DIFFERENT TYPES OF BALL ROLL

All bowlers will roll one of the following types of balls: straight ball; hook ball—full roller, semi-roller, semi-spinner, full spinner; back-up or reverse hook. Nearly all average and better-than-average bowlers will roll either the full roller or the semi-roller hook ball. The various types of rolls are pictured on the following pages.

Straight Ball

Figure 124 shows the straight ball. Notice that the hand is in back of, or behind, the ball as it is released. The thumb is pointed to approximately 11:30 o'clock as the ball is released, and the ball rolls down the lane like a wheel. The

124. The straight ball

bowler who rolls a straight ball must be certain to keep the thumb and fingers in these positions the instant the ball is released. It is easy for the thumb to slip beyond the 12 o'clock position, and the result is the undesirable back-up.

We recommend a straight ball for a bowler who lacks ball speed. The slower the ball and the lighter the ball, the more it will curve. Excessive curve makes accuracy a problem with a hook ball.

The straight ball should be rolled from the corner or outside angle, as in figure 124. Take advantage of the angle into the pocket to increase your strike chances. It is obvious that the ball will deflect less if it comes into the pocket from the outside angle (figure 124).

Full Roller

Approximately one percent of the top bowlers roll the full roller. It differs from the straight ball only in the position of the thumb and fingers at the instant the ball is released. The fingers lift the straight ball from behind (6 o'clock), whereas the fingers lift the full roller from the side (3 to 4 o'clock). The tape on the ball in figure 125 shows how the ball spins from right to left (3 to 9 o'clock). This lift from the side imparts the hook spin, which causes the ball to curve as it travels down the lane. Since the straight ball and the full roller differ only in the position of the thumb and fingers at the instant of release, it is obvious that the straight-ball bowler need only move the fingers around to the side of the ball as it is released in order to roll a hook ball. Notice that the ball track covers the full circumference of the ball, hence the name full roller. The track is from one-fourth to one inch wide (see figure 125), and is between the thumb and fingers.

125. Full roller

Semi-Roller

The semi-roller is the most popular of the hook balls. For the full roller, the axis of rotation is parallel to the lane surface. For the semi-roller (also known as a three-quarters roller), the axis is tilted somewhat, which causes the ball to roll on a track below the thumb hole. The semi-roller ball track will be less than the full circumference of the ball.

126. The semi-roller

Many bowlers consider the semi-roller to be the strongest hook ball, but it is the bowler's ability to impart split-second lift with good timing that determines the effectiveness of any hook ball. There are many weak and strong hook balls in both the full roller and semi-roller categories because of poor timing and poor ball-release techniques.

The difference in the full roller and the semi-roller stems from the lift imparted by the fingers. Notice the angle or direction in which the fingers apply the lift in the semi-roller (figure 126). Also notice how the wrist has a very slight "cocked" appearance that causes a tilt in the axis of rotation. By contrast, the full roller is given lift straight up. It is the angle of the fingers, with the wrist "locked" as the ball is released, that imparts the hook spin.

Semi-Spinner

Many bowlers use the term semi-spinner and semi-roller interchangeably. We use the term *roller* to refer to a ball in which the hook spin is applied by a lift with the fingers, with minimal or no wrist turn. For the *spinners,* the turn of the wrist is essential to apply a spin, with finger lift the secondary factor.

In any event, the difference between the semi-roller and semi-spinner can be seen when you compare the position of the ball track. For the semi-spinner, the wider or cone-shaped track is caused by applying more wrist turn, along with the lift by the fingers (figure 127).

It is natural for some bowlers to roll the wrist a bit counterclockwise as they release the ball. Others deliberately turn the wrist, as illustrated in figure 57, p. 65.

Full Spinner

This is the weakest of the hook balls, and it is not recommended. At best, it is only moderately effective on slow or running lanes and is practically lost on faster lanes and heavier pins.

127. The semi-spinner

The full spinner is released as illustrated in figure 128, with the wrist turning counterclockwise from directly on top of the ball. Little or no finger action is employed, and the ball travels down the lane spinning like a top. The only exceptions are some of today's pros who find the spinner the only possible shot in extremely slow conditions.

128. The full spinner

Why anyone chooses to roll the full spinner is puzzling. Perhaps bowlers who roll this ball are trying to roll the turn-and-lift type hook but have not developed the finger lift, only the wrist turn.

Back-Up and Reverse Hook

There is a distinct difference between a back-up and reverse hook. The back-up is actually intended to be a straight ball (see chapter 2), but because the right-handed bowler releases the ball with the fingers coming up a little to the left of center, the ball will fade to the right. The ball moving up to the right is similar to the reverse hook, but the reverse hook is thrown with a deliberate clockwise lift by the fingers. This is the same procedure that hook-ball bowlers follow for natural lift, except that the lift is from the opposite side of the ball.

We have known a few better-than-average reverse-hook bowlers. The bowler illustrated in figure 129 rolls a very strong ball. But the question is, why release the ball unnaturally when a natural hook lift is easier and so much better?

129. The reverse hook

How the Ball Rolls

The ball illustrated in figure 130 is a full roller. The ball track is between the two taped lines. The speed of this ball is medium.

Notice that the ball skids forward approximately 16 feet before any effect of the hook spin is noticed. This is much like a car skidding on ice, even though the front wheels may be turned. The skid is entirely the result of the momentum of the ball. The effect of lane friction begins to show in figure 130d, causing the track of the ball to turn and start into the forward roll. A semi-roller with average ball speed will also react in this manner (except for the power cranker, figure 130). Lane friction is a constant factor on the full length of the lane. Once the ball begins to change direction, the hook spin changes the direction at an ever-increasing rate. This accounts for the ball "breaking" from right to left in the last 10 to 20 feet of its journey. The hooking action of a bowling ball is similar to acceleration in physics. Once acceleration (hook spin) has started, the velocity (curve of the ball) will continue to increase.

A good hook ball delivered with average speed will generally make ten to fourteen complete turns after leaving the bowler's hand until it hits the pocket. The full roller illustrated in figure 130 makes twelve complete revolutions.

The ball illustrated in figure 131 is a cranker's semi-roller. Notice that the track, which is between the tapes, is below the thumb and to the side of the finger holes. The speed of this semi-roller is fast. These powerful hooks make fifteen to eighteen complete revolutions from the foul line to the pins.

Notice that the ball enters the pocket with more right-to-left angle than the hook ball with average speed. In contrast, however, because of the tremendous power and hook spin produced by the power bowlers (crankers), such as was illustrated in figure 58, the power ball will enter the pocket at practically the same right-to-left angle that it left the bowler's fingertips! As we mentioned previously, while the bowler who rolls an average hook "hopes for the best"—for a thin (light) pocket hit, the cranker ball overpowers the pins and piles them up on the side of the pin deck! Of course, the latter bowler must not only be very strong, but must also practice longer and harder to become accurate and consistent.

Bear in mind that with all things equal, the lane conditions, whether slick or slow, and their maintenance will also influence the roll of the ball—its revolutions—and the final pin-fall outcome, whether semi-roller, full roller or power ball.

15. EQUIPMENT

In every competitive sport it is necessary to have your own equipment, custom-fitted to your own dimensions, in order to achieve maximum performance. The golfer needs his or her own clubs; the baseball player a glove and a bat that feels just right; the bowler needs a ball that is custom-fitted to the hand. An ill-fitted bowling ball can cause physical damage such as blisters, swollen fingers and knuckles, and pulled muscles in addition to a sub-par performance. Every bowler

(a)

130. A full roller

(b)

(c)

(d)

(e)

131. A cranker's semi-roller

should purchase a custom-fitted bowling ball at the earliest opportunity. It is a small premium to pay for the extra enjoyment of the game. Bowling shoes and a bowling bag complete the outfit of very desirable custom equipment. Bowlers should wear loose, comfortable clothing that allows freedom of movement.

16. BALL PITCH

Many bowlers have a special grip that they have designed, and each has a reason for not using the conventional grip. Figure 132a shows the standard 3/8-inch pitch of the conventional three-hole grip. This is the design recommended by nearly all instructors, particularly for beginning bowlers.

Figure 132b shows a center drilling called zero pitch. The conventional drilling has a forward pitch 3/8 of an inch above the center of the ball. When you consider that the pitch of each hole in the ball may vary according to the particular whims of each bowler, you can readily see that it is possible to have an infinite number of different grips, each of which can be a perfect fit.

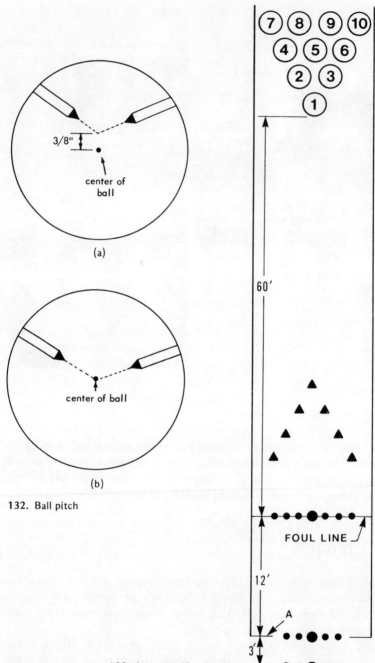

3/8"

center of
ball

(a)

center of ball

(b)

132. Ball pitch

133. Lane specifications

7 8 9 10
4 5 6
2 3
1

60'

FOUL LINE

12'

A

3'

17. BOWLING LANE SPECIFICATIONS

Figure 133 indicates briefly the bowling lane specifications. The lane is 60 feet from the foul line to the 1-pin, the head pin. The lane is 42 inches wide and the approach is 15-16 feet long (12 feet from the foul line to the line marked "A"). Lanes approved by the American Bowling Congress cannot be more than forty-thousandths (.040) of an inch higher or lower in any section or spot. The pins are set in a triangle, with each pin exactly 12 inches (center to center) from the pins on either side of it. A.B.C.-sanctioned pins must weigh from 3 pounds, 2 ounces to 3 pounds, 10 ounces. The pin positions are numbered as in the illustration.

18. LANE CONDITIONS

"Playing the lanes" is a skill acquired through years of bowling under various conditions. If the ball starts to hook sooner than usual or curves more than is normal, the bowler will refer to the lane as "slow" or "running." If the opposite situation is present, that is, the ball skids farther than normal and does not take a normal break, the lane will be referred to as "fast" or "holding." Most bowlers prefer to bowl on lanes that are shaded to the slow side.

What makes a lane fast or slow? In order to answer this question you must understand how the lane is constructed and maintained. The lane is made of boards 1 to 1-1/8 inches thick and 3 inches wide. These boards stand on edge. From the foul line, maple boards run out the distance of 16 feet. There they dovetail with pine boards of the same dimensions which run to within 1 foot of the head pin. At that point the pine boards again dovetail into maple boards, which form the pin deck, the portion of the lane on which the pins stand. A base coat of urethane is applied to the new lane, then two coats of urethane finish. When thoroughly dry, a coat of alley dressing is applied over the finish, and the lanes are ready for use. This alley dressing is nothing but a light coat of oil, which keeps the lane slightly lubricated so that the continual rolling of bowling balls does not wear through the urethane and into the boards.

If a lane is dressed too heavily with oil, or if you bowl on the lane immediately after this dressing is applied, the ball will skid further and resist the hook spin of the ball much more than if the ball were rolled on a lane that was free of oil. This dressing does not help to produce high scores if it is applied to the pin deck. The good bowler will never worry about fast or slick lane conditions at the head of the lane, as long as the last 10 to 20 feet and pin deck are not oily so that the ball will dig in when it reaches this critical area.

Assuming the lanes are properly maintained, other physical conditions cause lanes to vary from one to another. All boards of one type are not indentical. Some contain more pitch than others, some have a wide or open grain and thus absorb lane dressing rapidly, some have a narrow grain and resist absorbing so that the dressing will remain on top of them after it has been absorbed by other boards.

As a general rule, bowlers adjust for varying conditions in one of two ways. If the lane is slow or running, the right-handed bowler will either move the starting location a board or two to the left, or will move the target a board or two to the right to compensate for the additional hook. Of course, opposite adjustments are made for fast or holding lanes.

19. TEACHING SENIOR ADULTS

Bowling is prompted as a sport for all ages, and everyone can learn to bowl the correct and most comfortable way. The most important consideration for older adults who are learning to bowl is physical safety in order to avoid injury or strain. It is

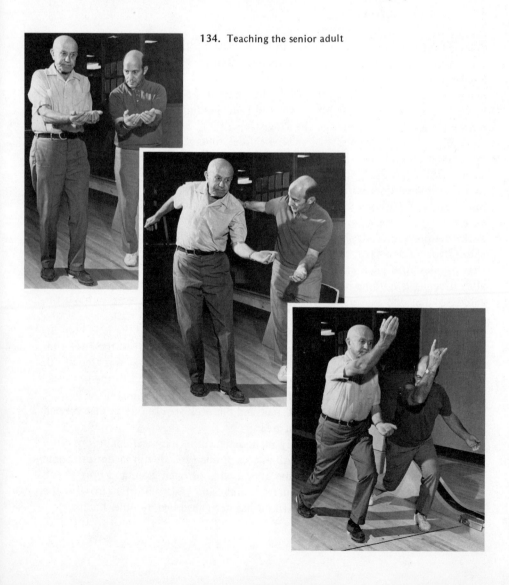

134. Teaching the senior adult

recommended that the instructor pay special attention to select a ball that has the appropriate weight for the bowler's strength, and that fits properly.

Figure 134 illustrates the best method for teaching senior citizens. The one-step delivery without the ball is the first technique. The instructor should make certain that the pupil understands the coordination of the step with the arm swing. After eight or ten complete simulated deliveries as shown, have the pupil try it with the ball. For the first attempt at rolling the ball, we suggest that the instructor remain at the bowler's side, as shown in figure 135.

Figure 135 shows the beginning bowler making the complete delivery on his own. Not only will he enjoy the sport, he will be able to score well with this one-step style. To change later to a three-step or four-step approach, refer to Chapter 1.

135. The first attempt at rolling the ball

20. TEACHING CHILDREN

Teaching boys and girls from the ages of six to ten is not a problem if you follow the procedure outlined in figure 136. We do not recommend teaching the approach immediately, no matter how light the ball may be.

Have the students pick up the ball with both hands, as shown in figure 136a and carry it to the foul line (figure 136b). Then, tell them to set the ball down and position themselves comfortably (figure 136c). Next, have them bring the ball back (figure 136d), then down and forward (figure 136e).

This method makes the swing easy for them, and they will learn to balance themselves properly and to face straight ahead at the same time they are knocking down pins, which is their biggest concern. Depending on their age and strength, the biggest problem is trying to keep the arm from twisting. If necessary, the instructor or a parent can hold the wrist as shown in figure 112d, p. 126. If the child has his or her own ball, this can be practiced at home. Keep the children bowling in this manner until they have developed better balance, and most important, the straight arm and hand position. Their scoring will improve automatically as they develop the proper approach form, (figure 139) and perfect balance and delivery form at the foul line (figure 138).

When this skill is mastered, the children are ready for the one-step delivery (figure 137) followed by the normal instructional sequence (three-step, four-step) described in chapter 1.

136. Teaching children to bowl

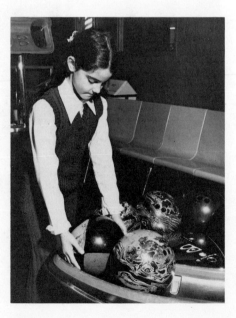

(a)

(b)

(c)

(d)

(e)

137. Learning the one-step delivery

138. Good delivery form

139. Proper bowling form

21. SCORING THE GAME OF TENPINS

Although scoring in bowling seems complicated to the beginner, it is quite simple after it is understood. Here are the symbols used in scoring:

 When the first ball in any frame knocks down all pins, it is a *strike* and is marked with an *X*.

 If all the pins are knocked down in two rolls, it is a *spare* and is marked with a slanted line. (The 7 is the number of pins knocked down with the first ball of the frame.)

 If a *split* is left after the first roll, it is marked with a circle.

 If the split is converted into a spare, it is marked with a slanted line through the circle.

 If no pins are hit on a shot, it is an error or a miss, and it is marked with a horizontal line. In this case, no pins were hit on the second roll, so the horizontal line is placed in the second box.

 If a bowler fouls, the score is an *F*, which is worth zero pins. (If scored on the first ball, the bowler nevertheless gets the pin fall for the second shot for that frame.)

 If the ball is rolled in the channel or gutter, the score is *G*, worth zero pins.

If you get a strike, your score will be ten pins—plus what you knock down on the *next two rolls* as a bonus in the strike frame. If you get a spare, you will receive ten pins—plus what you knock down on the *next roll* as a bonus in the spare frame. Remember, the first of the two small boxes within the frame records the pins knocked down with the first ball.

Following these simple rules of scoring, it is easy to determine your score in any frame. Here are some illustrations:

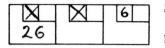

Scoring the first frame strike, remember it is worth 10 pins plus the score for the next *two* shots as a bonus.

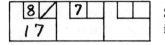

Scoring the spare made in the first frame, your score is 10 pins plus the score of the next shot as a bonus.

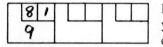

If you fail to knock down all ten pins with both rolls, your score is the total number of pins you knocked down in that frame.

Here is a sample of scoring a game or a "line":

1	2	3	4	5	6	7	8	9	10	TOTAL
9/	8 /	⊠	⊠	⊠	8/	⊠	⊠	7 Ø	⊠ ⊠ 8	
/8	27	57	85	/05	/25	/52	/72	/92	220	220

In the first frame, you knocked down all the pins with two balls, scoring a spare; show the spare symbol in the second small box. Do not record a score for the frame until after you roll your first ball in the second frame, because your score in the first frame will be ten for the spare plus what you get on the next shot as a bonus.

Your first ball in the second frame knocked down eight pins, so you add this to the ten for the spare, and you have eighteen in the first frame. Your second ball in the second frame got only one of the two standing pins, so you have an error (an open frame) and a total of nine pins for the frame. Eighteeen plus nine equals twenty-seven. Your first ball in the third frame knocked down all the pins so you mark a strike in the little box, but you don't add anything until you roll two more balls. In the fourth frame, you get another strike—making it a "double"—but you still show no score; remember, a strike gives you ten, plus your next *two* balls, so you have to wait for another ball.

In the fifth frame, you get a third strike, and three in a row is called a "turkey." Now we can add up the scoring in the third frame. Ten for the strike, plus and ten for the next two balls, making a total of thirty pins to be added to your score in the third frame, or 27 plus 30 equals 57. This is why 12 strikes in a row makes the perfect "300" game—it is simply 30 pins per frame for 10 frames. Notice how the score mounts when you bunch the strikes! In the sixth frame, you got eight pins with the first roll. Now you can add up your score for the fourth frame—it is ten plus the next two rolls (on which you got ten and eight). This makes 28 added to the 57 in the third frame, which makes 85 in the fourth frame. The conversion of the spare in the sixth frame gives you your score for the fifth frame (10 plus 8 plus 2 added to 85 makes 105 in the fifth frame). Follow the scoring for the rest of the game.

Notice that the tenth frame is the last frame to be scored. Any roll or rolls after the tenth frame are only to compute your bonus score for previous strikes or spares. In our example above, you got a strike on your first roll in the tenth frame. This strike gives you ten, plus two more rolls only. On the first extra roll you got 10 pins (a strike) and on the second extra roll, you got eight. This completes the game, as you do not get to roll at the two remaining pins.

How to Score a Foul

The foul line and what constitutes a foul are explained in chapter 1. Chapter 3 describes methods used for the correction of fouling. Now you must consider what the foul does to your score. When a foul is committed, the ball counts as a roll, but no pin fall is credited to your score. In other words, you treat a foul for scoring purposes the same way you would score a ball rolled in the channel—no score for that roll.

Handicaps for Scoring

As the word indicates, a handicap is an "equalizer," which enables the lower average bowler to compete with the higher average bowler. Without some type of handicap system, the higher average bowlers would win most of the time. All leagues are run on a handicap basis (with the exception of scratch leagues, which have no handicaps but must employ rigid maximum and minimum average requirements to ensure that individuals or teams are evenly matched). This is generally true of tournaments, although some are run on a classification basis, where bowlers are competing only against other bowlers with similar averages. For example, a tournament may run with A, B, C, and D classes, where C class would include all bowlers with averages between 160 and 169.

When organizing a handicap league, an arbitrary figure must be selected from which to figure the handicaps. The figure generally selected is 200, though it may be higher or lower. The figure selected is called the *scratch figure* for that league. A percentage of the difference between the bowler's average and the scratch figure is then allowed as handicap. The percentage generally used is two-thirds. For example:

Scratch figure	200
Bowler's average	179
Difference	21
Per game handicap	14 (if using 2/3 as the basis of handicap)

Each bowler's handicap is figured in a similar manner and is added to his or her total pins to determine the bowler's score for each game. The American Bowling Congress and the Women's International Bowling Congress (A.B.C. and W.I.B.C.) provide handicap charts at no charge. When figuring handicaps or averages, always drop any fractions. If the handicap figures to be 24-3/4 use 24 per game.

22. GLOSSARY OF BOWLING TERMS AND SLANG

A.B.C.	The American Bowling Congress.
A.J.B.C.	The American Junior Bowling Congress.
Alley	The lane.
Anchor man	The fifth or last person in the team line-up. Usually the best bowler.
Approach	The area on which the bowler takes the steps to the foul line; also the act of moving to the foul line to deliver the ball.
Arrows	The targets located 16 feet beyond the foul line. Synonymous with rangefinders and spot.
Baby-split	The 2-7 or the 3-10 split.
Back-up	A ball that fades to the right (for a right-hander) on its way down the lane.
Bedposts	The 7-10 split; also called "goalposts."
Big fill	A good count on the first roll following a spare—eight or nine pins.
Big four	The 4-6-7-10 split; also called "double pinochle."
Blind score	An absent bowler's score.
Blow	An error, a miss.
Bridge	The edge-to-edge distance between the finger holes.
Brooklyn	Hitting the left side of the head pin (for a right-hander).

Bucket   The 2-4-5-8 spare leave for a right-hander; 3-5-6-9 for a left-hander.

Channel   The troughs on either side of the lane. Also called "gutter."

Cheesecake   A lane that is very easy to score on; also called a "pie alley," or a "soft alley."

Cherry   Chopping off the front pin or pins on a spare shot.

Choke   To tighten up under pressure.

Count   The number of pins knocked down with the first ball.

Dead ball   A poorly rolled ball, one that deflects or bounces excessively.

Division boards   Where the maple boards and pine boards dovetail into one another about 16 feet from the foul line; also called the "splice."

Dodo ball   A term used in the old days for an illegal (weighted) ball.

Double   Two strikes in succession.

Dutchman   A 200 game made by alternating strikes and spares.

Error   A missed spare; same as a blow.

Flat apple or flat ball   Same as a dead ball.

Foul   Touching anywhere beyond the foul line with any part of the body or articles, such as clothing, that are attached.

Foul line   The black line separating the lane and the approach.

Foundation   Also a "good foundation," meaning a strike in the ninth frame.

Frame   One of the ten frames in a game; also called a "box."

Goalposts   The 7-10 split.

Graveyard   The toughest lanes on which to produce good scores.

Groove   Supposedly a "trough" in a lane all the way to the pocket, thereby making scoring much easier.

Gutter   The troughs on either side of the lane; also called "channels."

Handicap   As the name indicates, an adjustment in scores to compensate for unequal matching.

Head pin   The number one pin; the front pin.

Holding alley   Same as a "fast," "stiff," or "slick alley; one that cuts down on the amount of hook.

Jersey hit   Same as a Brooklyn hit.

Kegler   A bowler.

Kickbacks   The sideboards at the pit end of the lanes.

Kingpin	The five pin.
Leadoff	The first person in the line-up.
Lofting	Throwing the ball onto the lane from a position that is too upright thereby causing the ball to thump as it hits the lane.
Mark	Getting either a strike or a spare.
Nose hit	Hitting the head pin dead center on the first ball.
Open frame	A frame with neither strike nor spare.
P.B.A.	Professional Bowlers Association
Picket fence	The 1-2-4-7 or the 1-3-6-10 leave.
Pie alley	A "soft" alley; one on which it is easy to score.
Pitch	The angle at which holes are bored into bowling balls.
Playing the lanes	Adjusting to the conditions of a lane (e.g., fast or slow).
Playing the Tight Line	Releasing the ball so that its pathway follows a line from left of center (opposite for lefthanded bowlers) across the boards in the area of the third and center arrows and back to the strike pocket.
Pocket	The space between the 1-3 pins for right-handers; the space between the 1-2 pins for left-handers.
Powerhouse	A very strong hooking ball that seems to tear the pins apart.
Pumpkin	The opposite of a powerhouse; a very weak ball.
Railroad	A split leave, such as the 8-10, the 7-10, the 4-6, or the 7-9.
Return	The track on which the ball rolls back to the bowler from the pit.
Running lane	A slow or dry lane that allows more hook.
Runway	The approach area.
Scratch	Actual scores without handicap.
Sleeper	Any pin "hidden" directly behind another.
Soft alley	A lane that is easy to score on; a pie alley.
Spare	The score for knocking down all the pins with the two balls rolled in a single frame.
Split	Two or more nonadjacent pins left standing after the first roll, none of which is the head pin.
Squash	A dead or lifeless ball.
Stiff alley	A "fast," "holding," or "slick" alley; one that resists the ball's tendency to hook.
Strike	The score for knocking down all the pins with the first ball of a frame.

Strike out	To roll three strikes in the tenth frame.
Sweeper	A hook ball that works well and "sweeps" the pins off the lane into the pit.
Swinging the Ball	Releasing the ball so that its pathway moves toward the channel and then hooks back to the strike pocket.
Tap	A pin left standing after an apparently good strike hit.
Thin hit	A "light" hit; one that does not have enough "pocket."
Three points	Rolling the ball between the pins left in a split, and missing both of them; a reference to a football field-goal score. Also referred to as "field goal."
Turkey	Three successive strikes by one bowler in a single game.
Washout	The 1-2-4-10 leave for a right-hander; the 1-3-6-7 leave for a left-hander.
W.I.B.C.	Women's International Bowling Congress.
Working ball	A very effective ball having a lot of hook spin.
Y.B.A.	Youth Bowling Association